H. W. Hurst is a fully trained hypnotherapist
and psychotherapist of many years' experience
and is head of a private practice established in
the county of Cleveland. His research has already
featured in a programme for Tyne Tees
Television.

The Thousand Year Memory

H. W. HURST

SPHERE BOOKS LIMITED
30-32 Gray's Inn Road, London WC1X 8JL

First published in Great Britain by
Sphere Books Ltd 1983
Copyright © 1982 by H. W. Hurst

The author wishes to thank all those who took part in
the research programme, especially my five 'guinea-
pigs' and also Michael who co-ordinated the efforts of
the group.
My grateful thanks must go to Chris,
for his help and advice as editorial consultant,
throughout the compiling of the manuscript.

H. W. Hurst, D.H.P., M.A.H.P.

Stockton.

1982.

My book is dedicated
to
PETER
– who sowed the first seeds.

TRADE
MARK

Set in Times

Printed and bound in Great Britain by
Hunt Barnard Printing Ltd, Aylesbury, Bucks.

CONTENTS

1
Past Lives

Morag was a healer who spent her life preparing crude medicines from roots and herbs in the days of King Alfred. In fact, before Alfred was crowned he was once taken to Morag in the hope of relief from constant stomach pain, which often kept him awake at nights.

Centuries later a travelling player named Elizabeth De Bois reflected, on her death bed, that her life had not been a happy one. At fifty-four years old she still mourned the murder of her only lover. He was run through with a sword when she was just sixteen, but she remained faithful to him for the remainder of her grief-tinged life. That life was ended by a fever in the year 1267.

Ten year old Jeanette Cartier sailed from the French coast with her family to start a new life in England. For eight years she lived above the hatter's shop established by her uncle in the town of Bath. But when the family set sail on a second voyage, this time to America, Jeanette never lived to see either the coast of the New World or her nineteenth birthday. She was put to rest in the cold Atlantic along with many others, after an epidemic had raged through passengers and crew.

Compared with these three, Jane Martin had things easy. The daughter of a Member of Parliament, she had a comfortable childhood in a village near Gloucester at the beginning of the nineteenth century. Though she lived to be only forty, she had little misery in her life except when she was widowed by a fire which also claimed the life of her elder son.

The lives of these four women seem remote from our technological present. But what if I were to suggest that all these characters – or at least some undeniable part of them – had not only survived to this present day, but can all be found existing in one living woman? I do not propose to draw any rigid conclusions as to what part it is that remains or how it got there. But from mounting evidence, and after scrutiny which challenges all scepticism, I am compelled to come to the definite and rather disquieting conclusion that something inexplicable is present.

This woman's case is only one example of a phenomenon which can be found in almost everyone. Yet it is only recently that this startling key to the past has been discovered, and even more recently that anyone has taken its potential seriously enough to engage in organised research.

It is common practice among hypnotherapists treating a patient for an emotional problem to 'regress' that patient to an earlier time in his or her life. In the regressed state the patient can summon startling detail from many years back with a clarity that would be impossible for the conscious mind alone. Even right back to the point of birth no detail of environment or even emotion seems to have been lost in this great veiled storehouse of memory. One would expect the dawning of life to be the absolute terminus on this backward journey. Apart from the occasional claim of remembered sensation within the womb, what else can there be?

The surprising answer came at first by accident during normal therapeutic treatment. As a patient's past years were effortlessly peeled away, the sheet of his identity would suddenly be wiped clean and a new, totally different identity would emerge as clearly as the first. But the alarming thing was that the new identity would be of someone apparently long dead. Soon, more characters would appear in a long chain that seemed to take the patient back through the centuries, sometimes even thousands of years. The consulting room and couch are gone as the subject describes a village of wattle huts, a castle at banquet time or the clamour of swords in battle. The present day character melts away as a mediaeval minstrel tells of her pleasures and pains. What is not gone is that clarity which marks the unfolding of the subconscious memory. As the new environment emerges, its details are painted as vividly as the subject's most recent experiences back in the twentieth century. Listen to the almost pedantic detail Elizabeth De Bois puts into just a few seconds of her life:

'It is too smokey in the castle. It makes me cough ... the fire in the big fireplace ... burning logs ... It is very windy and it blows the smoke back in – cannot see across the hall sometimes. I will have to go to one of the halls near. There is more space in the hall – it is where the air comes in ... A bit colder. I am going down the staircase ... out to the tents. There are a lot of stairs and it is cold after you leave the hall. It is snowing a bit.'

Those were the words of a woman claiming to have been born in the year 1213. They were spoken to me on my couch in the year 1979.

My fascination for this curious phenomenon goes back even further than my professional connections with hypnosis itself, but it is not until much more recently that I have been in a position to contribute to the existing findings with a research project of my own. This book is the culmination of that project, which has led me over the past three years down many untrodden paths, some of which led to answers, but many of which pointed to more and bigger questions. I have learned all over again the truth of the adage of every researcher in any field – that the farther you travel, the more clearly you see what a long way is left to go.

The findings of the early researchers began to emerge over thirty years ago when one of the best known works, *The Search for Bridie Murphy* spread the word among the book-reading public. It told of an American girl who could describe in great detail her 'life' as an Irish peasant girl three centuries earlier. The findings pointed to a wholly new area of study that offered an enticing mixture of spiritual and historical interest backed up by scientific research that gave it a credibility lacked by so many of the other 'fringe' subjects. The human craving for some glimpse of eternity seems so blinding at times that many people abandon all rational demand for solid fact as soon as they catch the faintest glimpse of their goal. But here was something rare – a phantom that could be tied down. The attraction of the paranormal was being handed to the scientist in a package that did not dissolve at the first flicker of his probing spotlight.

A fine example of this was shown to me in one of my first personal contacts with the subject. In the late 1950s I met a Polish born hypnotist whose own brother was capable of speaking in a strange mediaeval dialect of French while in a deep trance state. Not only did his speech change dramatically in this state, but his face also became distorted until his features began to look quite different. The matter did not end there however; later investigation showed disturbing connections between the results and real recorded history. A photograph of the man's 'new' face showed a striking resemblance to the death mask of one of the Napoleons. The dialect used by the man could also be positively identified – it matched the forms of language from both the era and the region of France where the Napoleons were brought up.

I was becoming more and more intrigued by the subject, but at the time still had no professional links with hypnosis. It was through my work then, as a research executive with a pharmaceutical company, that I became more interested in psychology, and eventually I trained in hypnotherapy and psychotherapy. So now, armed with the necessary skills, I could at last make a reality of my urge to investigate past life regression fully.

The starting point for my own research was not the 'borrowing' of a few past patients already accustomed to hypnosis, but the gathering of a completely fresh group of volunteers. A working group of fifty was necessary, I decided, as I wanted to examine not only the phenomenon itself, but also the best practical method of selecting potential subjects. It was much later in the project, during the long weeks of historical cross checking, that from the group one subject emerged as giving the most interesting and rewarding results. It had been clear from the outset that one woman showed an excellent flair for recounting her many past lives while under hypnosis. But is was only in these latter stages that the positive confirmations from the archives began to set this woman head and shoulders above the others. Because of this, her names – for she has many names from her previous lives – will crop up again and again in this book as we examine the phenomenon via the clear accounts she has given us. One aid to historical research of this kind is the existence of notable personalities whose details were recorded on paper even in the days when literacy was found only among scholars and persons of office. With the support of such records I am grateful to my 'star' subject for Jane Martin.

I first met Jane when she was ten years old. That was in 1801, though the way Jane told me in vivid detail about all the things around her it could have been yesterday. From the couch of my consulting room, my 'star' subject was eased back gently into the character of Jane. As the transformation began to take place, her eyes suddenly saw a very different environment.

She is on her rocking horse in the nursery of her home in a Gloucestershire village called Berkley. It is May and she says she is happy. She tells us the name of her home and that she has lessons by private tuition. I ask her where her father is.

'He is away.'
Do you know where?
'Gone to London.'
What does he do in London?
'Parliament.'

She goes on to tell me that she thinks he is the M.P. for Gloucester.

This instant foothold into the archives showed at first a disappointing dead end, with no member for Gloucester ever listed under that name. But there was a member for Tewkesbury, just twenty miles away, by the name of James Martin. According to the records, he took up office in 1776.

At twenty-five Jane is living at a place she says is called Rowden Farm and is in Devon. But here she introduces us to a perplexing aspect of the search for factual confirmation of these historic scenarios. After telling us of their home at Rowden Farm, the transcript goes on to say that their house burned down, killing her husband and son, when she was thirty-two. Rowden Farm still exists today, exactly where Jane says it is: but no record can be found of the fire which, Jane claims, gutted their home. Again and again, among statements verifiable from books and archives, the subjects mention places which defy any attempt to trace them. Indeed, in some cases the evidence points to the possibility that they did not exist. But how and why does such apparent fantasy emerge along with sound fact and where documented evidence confirms other details as accurate? Could it be that we have two phenomena in one – a genuine recollection with apparently needless fiction embroidering the facts? What could be the reason for such apparent wanderings from the truth? Perhaps we should bear in mind that if this is a genuine memory of some kind it would be asking a lot to expect infallibility. Maybe the untruths simply slip in to embellish some threadbare patch where even this astonishing phenomenon of recall has failed. As anyone who has spent any time in a court of law will know only too well, even the conscious memory not only plays similar tricks all the time but also paints such convincing pictures as to make a completely independent witness with no reason to lie swear on the Bible that every word is beyond question.

But, to return to the traceable evidence, I have found that it shows its real strength not in its accuracy but in its obscurity. It is the tiny everyday details of lives past that would probably never even come to the attention of the historians, let alone interest them. Jane Martin's story illustrates this point. What this girl has retained in her 180 year memory seems the very antithesis of the historian's meat. The girl described the environs of Rowden Farm as if it were outside my consulting room window, yet in recalling that her father is an M.P. she did not even know his constituency. It is of course a fair assumption that these are the patterns a ten year old child's memory would follow. But that would only support the theory that what we are hearing is in some way the genuine recollection of a child, rather than a trick of the present day subconscious. Would not our modern subject's subconscious memory arise from some long forgotten but real experience in this life? And if so, would not that memory, say of an ancient newspaper cutting, or passing glimpse of a television feature, be more likely of major incidents or personalities? This is only conjecture, but it is still food for thought. Another subject says of her wedding day 'lovely, lovely Thursday', then gives on request the exact date in the mid nineteenth century. It took pages of arithmetic, sorting back through the years and leap years, to reach a conclusion that had come instantly to her – that date was indeed a Thursday.

Then there is the opposite of the tendency for trivia. What happens when a subject quotes the kind of fact which should be easy to trace but cannot be traced? Obviously, we say, a dead end for the researcher. But it was one such 'dead end' in my investigations that led a near abortive search into a more exciting discovery than many of the obviously positive findings. Did nineteenth century London have a Ludgate Street? Every scrap of documentation we could find at the time led us to say no. Yet a character emerged through regression claiming to live in Ludgate Street at that period. There was a Ludgate everything else, the archives tell us – Hill, Passage, even Circus – but no Street. Until, that is, a friend of mine was staying at a country hotel on holiday and an old grandfather clock caught his eye. The ornate clock face was clearly marked with the maker's name and the address of his business. The clockmaker's shop was in Ludgate Street.

What are we to make of it all? Are we witnessing reincarnation? Or can it be some genetic memory buried in the junk-filled attic of the memory where only modern hypnotic methods can reach far enough to blow off the dust? Or is it simply some trick of the subconscious, throwing out distorted memories to play silly games with the curious?

My choice of semantics in the following pages may seem to beg the question, but references to 'past lives' or 'earlier lives' and so on are not meant as a conclusion on my part that what we are witnessing is reincarnation. I have set out to record this project, not to draw a final conclusion, but instead to weigh up all the existing possibilities in the light of my findings. However, the phrases describe in a neat little package what one might more pedantically call 'phenomena taking the form of apparent past lives'. And only when we have investigated the phenomena to the full can we seriously consider why they occur, and what they really are.

2
Methodology

A woman lies on the couch, slipping gently into a deep trance. It is the beginning of my project and the woman is Sheila, who will later become my 'star' subject. Although not yet fifty, she has a head of completely white hair.

In the three years since that time, Sheila underwent an inexplicable transformation in her appearance almost as staggering as that of the Polish Napoleon. At each successive session, the personality of Sheila stood back as Jane, Jeanette, Elizabeth and finally Morag took the stage. Then, as this went on for several weeks, something strange began to happen. Reaching out from her crown came a new growth of coarse black hair quite unlike any hair she had ever had. In past years she had been dark – but this was black. And it was not only the colour but also the texture that had changed. The softness of her hair gave way to a wiry coarseness that grew in with the new colour until together they gave the appearance of a skullcap through which the snowy pre-regression growth seemed to protrude. And now that the present research is over Sheila's other selves are allowed to rest in the shadows again, this curious blackness is fading as her soft white hair grows back.

The human head grows about 120,000 hairs at one time. In looking back at this strange phenomenon manifested in Sheila, I cannot help but feel that every single hair on her head was trying to tell me something.

Our eyes may be the easiest sensory organs to amaze and such changes in physical appearance make a deep impression on the witness. But more staggering than these were the revelations that came from the mouths of the subjects, and the uncanny accuracy with which some of this information checked out. That same head which from the exterior performed spontaneously this bizarre party trick revealed from within a vast library of fact that would have taken a trained historian months of archive-scouring to glean. The next logical question of the sceptic would be – how much history lies in that same head in its normal state of everyday consciousness? Sheila is by no means an academic, her only conscious brush with history being an unenthusiastic smattering of text-book Tudor dating back to her school days. Could such a woman really have come up with a detailed account of Alfred the Great's appearance right down to his family, his personal appearance and even his intestinal battle for health? It is difficult to take seriously the shouts of the cynic that she, even on a subconscious level, simply made the lot up. Too much of Morag's story stands up to deep scrutiny for us to give much credit to this theory. Another theory proves much harder to shoot down, but with each new piece of research that is done, the odds against it become longer and longer. This is, that we are hearing not some genuine memory of a past life, but a compilation of random present-life memories cobbled together into a dramatised cameo with the subject at the centre. It is beyond question that the subconscious mind has far greater powers of retention than the conscious, as is shown in the present-life regressions of everyday, but does that go far enough to explain what we are seeing? Taking King Alfred again as our example, the leader's reputation has earned him many a place in everything from children's stories to works by the most serious historical students. Much of Morag's tale could at a pinch have been bolted together from deeply retained snippets gleaned from every television series and comic adventures strip ever to feature Alfred. But how many of such mass appeal outlets care to mention that our bold hero was kept awake by a troublesome digestive tract? I personally know of none, and for that matter neither does the fully conscious Sheila. Indeed, such detailed and intimate information appears to have no outlets at all until one reaches the most academic of his biographies.

But the time for speculation will come later. Such a subject set a myriad puzzles to perplex anyone who dares to delve, but we cannot discuss these fully until we have considered the evidence.

*

It became clear that any new project setting out simply to extend the existing knowledge would not be new at all. It would simply saddle any interested party with the need for a slightly bigger library to house the same amount of information. A fresh work needed a fresh approach: it had to add direction to this existing wealth of potentially fascinating material. It was clear that if I was to do anything constructive to exploit this potential I would have to be prepared to do some deep digging.

So, from the very outset, the goal was a two-fold one – to examine the subject and add to the existing bank of knowledge, but also to study and eventually improve upon the way it had been approached in the past. The first need to show itself was for a completely purpose-built and structured project on past life regression that was actually begun with that intention in mind. Much of the previous research had been of limited value, resulting as it did from stumbling on the ability to regress and only then, after accumulating a file of case notes, deciding to write up the results.

As I said earlier, the starting point had to be the gathering of a large and fresh working sample of volunteers. This had to be big enough to exclude irregularities from the point of view of consistency even after an initial heavy pruning for the purpose of streamlining the project. For, although the results were later to show that virtually everyone had these enigmatic experiences from the past, the ease with which they could be coaxed out into the light varied enormously from one subject to the next. The sample also had to be fresh, because I wanted each one to start with the clean sheet of complete inexperience and no more prior knowledge of the subject than the small amount common to the public nowadays. Thanks to the publicity given to earlier life regression in the past, I had no difficulty in getting an ample crop of volunteers. In fact, a single press advertisement produced no less than eighty, of whom fifty were prepared to undergo regression. Of the other thirty, all those who followed through their initial enquiry were able to lend a hand with the equally invaluable task of tackling the 'backroom work'. For the regressions themselves were only a fraction of the project, the main part being the laborious but rewarding documentation and its validation.

By this time, I had already spent a number of months gathering the results of previous research in the field and speaking to as many of the people involved as possible. Also, I had prepared a structure and protocol for the various stages of the research that would hopefully support the project with a solid backbone of consistency. But what was to be done with my harvest of volunteers? By the time a full dossier could be prepared on every past life of each one, including full historical validations, we would probably all be long dead. Perhaps in that state of death we will be furnished automatically with all the answers, but I could not wait that long. With such an ample field to reap, it was possible – and indeed necessary – to focus my attention on those subjects with the greatest ability, not only to regress, but to furnish checkable data. Yet, while being able to specialise on a select few, I would still have the entire team to fall back on for a broader picture of the phenomenon as a whole.

The first major hurdle to be overcome was the distillation process itself. As the idea of handpicking subjects from scratch was completely unprecedented, I had to work completely in the dark and devise whole new processes of evaluation and selection. The ideal would be to use only the very best deep trance subjects, then to construct a skeleton biography of each one in every past life experience. This would then give me a framework of information which would be of enormous help in the building of each full dossier. Such an ideal seemed impossible to achieve as I looked forward at the beginning of the project. But with a lot of thought, much planning and considerable adaptation from existing standard hypnotic techniques, that ideal was achieved.

The first whittling down process was the assessment of each volunteer's relative potential as a deep trance subject. The regression of a subject into an earlier life requires a far deeper trance than, say, an ordinary session of hypnotherapy. It would be possible with extensive conditioning to achieve the necessary depth in anyone. But what was the point? While time was at a premium, I had an abundance of subjects just waiting for some selection process to identify the elite.

The method I devised was based on fundamental statistics and simply required a measure of the parameters I was seeking, then some means of expressing the result in numerical form. The method, which proved extremely reliable, took only about an hour per subject and produced a figure which could be instantly compared with the results of the other subjects. While this figure was, in itself, quite meaningless for a single subject, the whole set could be put into one league table with the lowest numbers at the top ready for the best ten performers simply to be creamed off. These ten formed the middle level in what would eventually become a pyramid with the back-up team across the broad base and Sheila at its apex.

Eventually, five parameters were adopted as the basis for the guide number. The first two tests, to measure the suggestibility of each subject, were made outside hypnosis. But the volunteers were put into light hypnosis for the other three which were designed as a guide to estimating how easily each could be put into deep trance. For those familiar with hypnosis, the five parameters were: the times required to achieve eye catalepsy, hand-levitation by suggestion, eye closure using a direct gaze technique, establishment of Ideo-Motor Signal (a most useful tool which I was to apply many times during the project) and Reciprocal Inhibition (in this case timing up to the achievement of a present life regression). The five recorded times, each measured in seconds, were then simply added together and the result divided by five. In cases where one of the figures was over five minutes it was discounted as irrelevant and the result instead divided by four.

Now the quality of my raw material was assured and it was almost time to open the curtain on history at last. But, even now, I was not satisfied with simply pulling that curtain right back: there was still more spade work to be done. Up to this point, there was no way of gathering information on these lives-before-birth without full regression, which can be very time consuming.

So I set about devising a quick and accurate cataloguing process which would obviate the need for regression at this stage. All I needed to know in advance of the regression stage were the basics of each life such as the given name, the dates of birth and death (the latter being very important for ethical reasons, which I shall come to later) and the correct sequence of lives.

The answers to the questions 'have you lived before?' and 'how many lives have you had?' were obviously the first ones I had to elicit and this is where Ideo-Motor-Signalling comes in again. This involves placing the index finger of the non-dominant hand under the control of the unconscious mind. By this means, the humble digit can be made to twitch dramatically and form a simple but direct means of setting up a working relationship with the unconscious mind. Thus, without involving the infinite complexities of the human speech, a massive amount of buried information can be unearthed. I found that by reducing every question to one requiring a yes/no answer the potential was virtually limitless, but it is even possible to take its versatility one step further. By reducing the entire alphabet to the same kind of binary limits, the subject's one finger can compose whole sentences without the mouth uttering a syllable. However, this is clearly a laborious method of gaining information, so I terminated I.M.S. interviewing after a simple count of lives in each subject and returned to the drawing board for an easier route towards the remaining data.

The next step brings us to the ethical point I mentioned. Imagine a cannon, not the modern variety with every built-in control, but the original monolithic cored-iron thunderer. It could be aimed to the left or right with surprising accuracy but in terms of distance its aim was apalling. You could fire the great ball down the line, but only trial and error would tell you where along that line it would land. And so it had always been with past life regression. We all knew where to aim but, as with the cannonball, how far away we would land was a matter of complete chance. It was a serious problem, which not only wasted valuable time but also raised a disquieting question of ethics. For the usual point of landings though unpredictable, was far from random. In the majority of cases, the subject would free-float gently up and down the time scale, then suddenly land at some point of high drama. Occasionally these would be joyous moments – pleasant occurrences from the past whose emotional content had the power to anchor the wandering mind. Childbirth and wedding days were common in this category: but these happy recollections were in the minority. More often, screams of agony would tear at the peace of the researcher's consulting room as a life was summoned, only to end within minutes in excruciating pain. Or a subject would choke and gasp as the lungs recited the horror of death by plague. Indeed, the sweat and screams of such ordeals have almost become the trade mark of past life regression wherever it has come into the public eye. The sound of a Roman soldier writhing in the death throes of a sword wound may be a great crowd-puller, but those tortures are very real to the subject. Years, even centuries, may have passed since the blood flowed, but what we see and hear happening on the couch is more than any historical play-acting. The emotions become so all-consuming during the reliving of these agonies that we must stop before going any further and ask ourselves a very serious question. Is it humane to force any thinking entity through such terror for the second time simply because some scientific Peeping Tom fancies a glance into that person's past? It is a question which could entangle philosophers for hours eternal. When does a vivid recollection of unpleasantness actually become equally un-pleasant in itself?

I could afford neither the time nor the qualms. A steering mechanism must be found for our erratic cannonball, and it must be found at the beginning of the project and not at the end.

The best way of avoiding such death-bed dramas would obviously be to know in advance of any regression exactly when death occurred and thus steer round the dates. But this had never been done before without the use of full regression, and I had other reasons besides compassion for wanting to avoid regression at this stage. Firstly, the group creamed from the screening process was still a little too top heavy to put each through a full programme. But also, I wanted to gain information outside regression which could be used to cross check the facts gleaned later. It was important for me to know, for example, just how many lives each subject had to offer, as in the normal free float methods it would be quite possible to skip one or more lives altogether. Also, the larger group would form more watertight proof that no two lives from one subject ever overlap chronologically. This is a particularly strong weapon against the rather illogical claim by some sceptics that the phenomenon is composed entirely of unconscious fantasy.

As with the use of I.M.S., I set to work again along the lines of adapting some of the existing tools of hypnotherapy to help me out in the cataloguing. I did not know at this stage even whether any more information about past lives was available at the level of relatively light hypnosis, but decided to adapt four techniques which I thought might give me the answer:

1) Automatic writing. You only have to read the phrase and immediately it conjures up visions of seances and spirit mediums. But it can take many more forms than this alleged bridge across the spirit void. It can also reach within the mind, and touch just the spot we are looking for – not the deep and elusive spot where the entire earlier life memory lingers, but a more easily attainable point on the fringes, which is shallow enough to reach without great effort while still holding the brief skeleton of information we need.

2) Automatic Voice Control. This is similar to automatic writing except that the speech mechanism is put under the control of the unconscious instead of the writing hand.

3) Experimental regression by free float. I tried this, the most conventional method, to see whether it would prove practicable despite my earlier feelings. It was not.

4) Guided Visual Imagery. This was the method I found to be the most accurate and productive of the four, although the first two had also produced results to a lesser degree, G.V.I. is a means of harnessing the part of the mind where the five senses are linked with the imagination. We all know the phrase, 'the mind's eye', but perhaps do not realise that the mind also has, in the same way, a nose, tongue, ears and fingertips. By flooding all these senses in the hypnotised mind with strong and pleasant stimuli, it is easy to catch the unconscious by surprise and uncover otherwise much guarded secrets. The most common way is to put the mind on a short fantasy journey towards a book in a library. At each step, more and richer sensory details are implanted – the smell of flowers in the library garden, the feel of the sun-warmed path under bare feet, and so on – until the subject reaches the book. The subject is then told the title of the book which relates directly to the aspect being probed, and then, while the unconscious is still off guard, he or she can open the imaginary book and quite easily read its contents aloud.

With this short-cut to the mental filing cabinet of past lives, I could then elicit from my top ten subjects the dates of birth and death in each life as well as other basic details such as names, sex and cause of death. This not only provided the solid structure upon which the whole project could be based but also meant that, with the bulk of the three year study still ahead of me, the enormous problem of free-float had been eradicated. From then on, no one need ever 'die' on my couch again.

I have already mentioned that almost everyone has these memories of apparent past lives. They may be more or less reluctant to surface depending on the particular subject but they are there in almost every case. I say almost every case for my group did manage to produce one volunteer with not a scrap of recollection from past lives. Not a very interesting case, you might think, yet this solitary soul (literally, it seems, as well as in the vernacular) had a staggering contribution which answered one question before I had even thought to ask it. Think back to my introduction of Sheila and her past lives. Each death was followed by many years before the rebirth into the next tangible body. Consider this brief extract from the interview with Jeanette Cartier, Sheila's third life. She has already died on that ill-fated sea voyage, yet some form of consciousness still speaks to us.

HH	How long have you been dead?
Jeanette	A week.
HH	What have they done with your body?
Jeanette	In the water.
HH	Who dropped your body in the water?
Jeanette	Sailors.
HH	Did many people die?
Jeanette	Yes.
HH	What do you feel? Can you see anything?
Jeanette	Cold and green.

We know from this and many other examples that the mind retains an unconscious memory of this inter-life limbo as well as of each separate life. In some cases the sensations are of being trapped in or near an extinct body; in others they are of peace and pleasure expressed in some aesthetic form such as floating over water into the sunset. But the question answered by our single-life volunteer is – does the memory uniting this long string of recollections have more awareness about the realities of the phenomenon while it is dissociated from mortal flesh than when it takes up residence again? Clearly few of us in our present lives would claim any conscious insight into what it's all about, but does that unconscious, continuous memory know more than it is telling? The volunteer not only answered this question but did so in such a chilling way that for a moment it took my breath away. She was not regressed but replying under hypnosis to my preliminary questions in the form of automatic writing.

Ballpen and paper in hand and with eyes wide open, as is possible in this state, she gave us this staggering insight from deep within:

HH   How many lives have you had before?
Subject   (*no answer*)
HH   Have you lived before?
Subject   No.
HH   Will you have other lives when this present one ends?
Subject   Yes.
HH   How long will elapse after your death before you are
            born again?
Subject   Forty or fifty years.
HH   Where will you be during that time?
Subject   In the spirit world.
HH   Where are you from?
Subject   Infinity.

This brief intercourse offered a gem of knowledge that had never been uncovered before. To the very best of my recollection, it was the first time ever that a subject in the hypnotic state had actually divulged abstract knowledge from outside the sphere of any mortal life. Peaceful scenery or the stifling loneliness of burial, are, as I said, fairly common. But this was something quite different.

Having satisfied myself that the virgin soul had nothing further to offer, I waited hopefully as I put each volunteer through the same tests, but to no avail. She was the only one with an answer to these questions. But even so, and considering how far from prolific she was, I was well pleased with the small shaft of light she had thrown onto the inquiry.

But not all the experiences of the early processing stages were so profound – far from it, in fact, as another female volunteer showed in a delightfully amusing way. As she was being eased into hypnosis by the usual practice of gentle, lilting speech, her voice suddenly bellowed from the couch, 'You'll have to speak up – it's my batteries'.

What could this be? Had she spontaneously regressed into a past life as a robot? But no, the subject slowly raised her hand to point at a small hearing aid with, we assume, fast fading power. I have hypnotised many hundreds of patients over the years, but this was the first time I had to induce this most relaxed state by yelling like a sergeant major.

With the screening of subjects well under way, I had not planned to begin the regressions proper until all the preliminary work was completed. But, as with early past life regressions, the first in my project came by accident. During one part of the processing I have already described, I asked each subject under hypnosis to regress to an earlier time in their present life. I chose the most consistent technique, which is to drift the subject back to lock on a particularly happy moment. All went as planned at first, and each volunteer complied as I recorded the necessary data from this exercise. But then one woman, with no other directing from me, slipped spontaneously into another character who, it turned out, had been dead for some time. Why did she skip her entire present life without any apparent external stimulus? The answer did not come until another woman showed exactly the same startling tendency to by-pass her own life. I did not know at the time that the women in their present lives were actually sisters and had both suffered wretched childhoods. Their lives had yielded not enough joy in youth for them to package into what might be called a happy memory. To them, the search for joy meant a search beyond the womb and conscious memory, so if they were to comply with my instruction they had no choice but to regress into an earlier life.

The experience of speaking to these very first voices from the past gave me renewed encouragement to tackle the final step prior to the full regression stage. Up to that point each individual researcher had apparently adopted his own method of actually regressing a patient (I say patient, not volunteer, as almost all previous regression exercises have developed from hypnotherapy sessions). Probably in most cases the method has carried on from the individual's particular style of hypnotherapy. I knew of four styles thought to be in common use, although most practitioners are secretive about their methods, and each one was put through the same formal scientific examination as every other unknown quantity in the project. I found a clear lead from one of these methods which could be increased even further by a little adaptation and then settled on that one for the entire future programme of regressions. The methods themselves are based simply on the semantics used by the practitioner and would mean little to the unqualified reader.

Having cleared the project of the need to force the volunteers through agonising death scenes, we did not miss out on any of the detail – or even the drama – of the deaths and their circumstances. The only reason that had forced past researchers to approach a death in this way was that they did not know in advance when that death occurred. Like a blind man walking towards a wall, they had to carry on forward until they bumped their noses against it. But now that the problem no longer existed for me, I could use the very accurate advance warning of death dates to land each subject at the other side of the fatal moment. Each one could be taken through life in five year jumps, then hopped neatly over the final agony. Beyond the void, all of life's emotions are gone, as the later interviews show, but the memory remains intact. The place of burial, the circumstances of death, even the culprit in the cases of murder can be reviewed quite dispassionately.

See how this is borne out in the closing moments of one of the interviews made possible by this method. The subject is no longer the axis of the sad scene; merely the story-teller. Here Mary Morrison, the first of three past lives produced by my subject Tina, has not the chance to wait around for her own funeral because of the time which passes before her body is discovered. The continuing part of her must move on now that starvation has ended her life, but not before she has had time to comment on the sight of her own body:

Mary There is no money at all ... I can hardly get out of the
        chair ... Starving.
(*Then taken to the time after death.*)
        She is still there ... she is ... in the chair.
HH   Your body? Is it dead?

Mary Yes.
HH   You have left the body. Has anyone found her yet?
Mary No.
HH   How long ago did she die?
Mary Hours.
HH   When did you leave her body?
Mary Don't know. Moving forward.

The one exception I have found to the extremely useful conquest of earthbound emotion is where fresh displeasure is incurred actually after death. Obviously, there is little one can do to upset a corpse – except perhaps to bury it. Normally, by the time the remains are ready for burial, this spirit or whatever it is that we have caught is out of the flesh and able to watch from close by, but in one case from my records a woman showed extreme disgust at being covered by the earth. She was obviously a little late in leaving the body, as was Jeanette Cartier, who felt the cold, green sea enveloping her.

At this point, I should perhaps explain the high incidence of women among my volunteers. At a very early stage in the screening process, women showed a distinct edge over the men in my league table of usefulness as deep trance subjects. Indeed, when I settled on a final core of the best five subjects to form the basis of the project and this book, every one of the five was female.

For every one past life ever unlocked by any researcher, there has probably been at least one living person spending ten times as long in the archives and parish registers. These laborious hunts for footholds of fact to link with the regressions are the most obvious route to enlightenment on the nature and validity of the elusive What? But there are other, as yet untrodden paths where equally useful clues may be waiting. The facts within the spoken word have been examined in the context of where they might fit in the pattern of history. What about the visual images that go along with the words in the memory? Or what about leaving history aside for the moment and examining the direct relationship between the modern-day subject and his or her 'family within'?

To take the first point – yes it is possible to have these verbal snatches of the past embellished with illustrations. Sometimes these could be produced by subjects while under hypnosis, but in other cases the memory of the regression interview and the visions it can summon remain vivid in the mind's eye when normal consciousness is resumed. It was after my subject Tina had regressed to her life as Mary Kaye and been subsequently returned to the present that I first saw this. Tina immediately on opening her eyes asked for paper and a pencil. The house she drew in outline was the one she had just described from the seventeenth century as her home.

Drawing with the eyes of the past also figures strongly in examining the relationship between past characters and their present counterparts. We have known throughout the years of documented findings all about thousands of past lives called up by hypnotic regression. We have dwelt for hours on the accuracy of every tiny factual statement and cheered every bull's-eye when they checked out. But why not turn the inquiry to a deeper level, and examine the actual character that is at the centre of each of these scenes? It seems doubly odd that this facet of research has never been examined before, if one considers the intimate links between hypnotherapy – the occupation behind most regression work – and psychology. Perhaps it is because any findings from such a probe were thought to have less potential as attention-grabbers than some of the more dramatic validation discoveries. Despite this, the belief in a changing character is as old as – and indeed closely linked with – the doctrine that the dead will return as flesh. To millions of people throughout the world, particularly in the Asiatic religions, a gradual purification of character in progressive lives is seen as the very reason for reincarnation. In the philosophy known as Karma, the person in one life is confronted with the faults and errors of his previous life, so that he may see the flaws from both sides as part of his conditioning for eternity.

It would of course be a mammoth task to quantify the good and evil within an individual, and completely impossible to do so while taking into account the specific mores of each culture and time, which define the interpretation of the morals themselves. But what about the far more fundamental yardstick of character in the parameters seen by the psychologist? Introversion and extroversion, hopes and fears, likes and dislikes are just some of the characteristics we consider in assessing the people around us. Ask someone about a facet of his personality and he may answer 'I've been like that for as long as I can remember'. I can now tell you that he is wrong. Oh, he may have been that way for as long as his conscious mind can remember, but I have found that the picture changes dramatically as soon as he is given the ability to look back beyond the womb.

I began to examine this difference by compiling a standard test questionnaire and, by that, analysing the five core subjects in their present life. The questions were similar to accepted test papers and at this stage the examinations were made outside hypnosis. The next step was to allow as much time to elapse as possible before putting the past lives through the same questions; thus the possibility of conscious intervention was minimised. I chose to examine what was in most cases the most recent of the past lives so that the cultural differences between that and the present would be minimal and the questions thus more relevant. For reasons of consistency, the subjects were each regressed to a time when their chronological age was the same as their present age. And this is why the most recent life was not used in absolutely every case. In the event of the most recent life ending too soon, then the most recent one where they survived to their present age was used instead.

The results were that a staggering seventy-seven per cent of the characters were totally different in the subsequent life. This figure is even larger if you consider that all personalities, even of different present-day people, have their similarities merely by the laws of average and chance. So much so, in fact, that it seems quite safe to state that, in terms of personality, every step back in time produces a totally different person. They are as different within from the living subject as their environment is from the subject's environment.

The full analysis of the personality profiles I will go into in much more depth later in the book, but this phase of the project produced one perplexing offshoot which has nothing directly to do with the personalities at all. Among the set verbal questions was a test in which the subjects were each asked to draw a person of their own sex and one of the opposite. For the personality test this was simply compared with the drawings of a man and woman by the past character. Such drawings contain all sorts of clues which can be interpreted by the psychologist. But could a psychologist – or, for that matter, anyone else – explain how a character from regression can draw something that the present day subject cannot even see? For a subject needing powerful spectacles for any close work seemed mysteriously rid of this myopia when regressed, and drew with the naked eye what would be little more than a fuzzy outline to the same subject outside hypnosis. Even more common than that was the phenomenon of the regressed person showing far more artistic dexterity than in present life.

Slowly but surely the evidence from this and many other fine details is piling up in favour of the belief that there is something very real and very positive at the heart of all this – that this is not pure fantasy or mental trickery. But within that pile of evidence, how do those subordinate piles stand which pull our beliefs towards the various theories? I believe it will be a very long time before any one of those piles grows big enough to topple all the others around it. But in subsequent chapters I have laid out the evidence of my own findings over the three years through the routes opened by the five subjects at the centre of the project. All that remains is for you to apply your own judgement to them!

3

Tina – Daughter of Two Captains

In the three years of the research programme, I have been privileged with the rare friendship of dozens of characters from ages past. The strange medium of past life regression has introduced me to a whole spectrum of personalities I could never have hoped to meet by any other means. The happy and the sad, the wealthy and the humble, the good and the not-so-good have all emerged from their sleep of the centuries to greet me. Many have poured out their hearts to me and told of their secret joys and fears. And who can blame them? If these characters are, as they claim, genuinely from past history, then it was their first chance of a chat in hundreds of years. And of all these people, I found no character more endearing than Sadie Jewkes.

Born in 1871, she was christened Sarah but her pet name seems to suit her personality far more. She has the air of one of those flamboyant, impish girls who is never at a loss to raise the spirits of those around her. Yet when sadness comes, as it did in her short but fruitful life, she is not afraid to make the listener privy to her deepest thoughts. Sadie is the most recent of three lives to be presented to me by Tina, one of the volunteers, a married school teacher, age thirty-five at the time of regression, with no children. She has lived her entire present life in the north east of England, though all her past lives seem to have taken place in the south and south west. Over a span of slightly more than two centuries she has been the daughter of two captains – one of the sea, one an army captain who was later disgraced for embezzlement. She has died in a riding accident, passed away bedridden at the age of sixty-five and spent her dying years in seclusion to hide her small-pox-ravaged features from the world. As one life ended, she reflected on the sad irony that she was married and buried in one year. The same guests gathered at the same church, but the second time the women's tears were not shed in happiness for the bride. In another life she married her way out of poverty into the luxurious carved wooden bed of a merchant. But there was no love there, and when his life ran out so did the money, and she was a pauper again.

But let us first meet Sadie, Tina's most recent life with its twenty-one years of bliss and agony from 1871 to 1892:

HH   Tell me what is happening to you. Where are you?
Sadie I am in bed.
HH   Are you ill?
Sadie I have got – well – a fever.
HH   How old are you?
Sadie I think I am nine.
HH   Is your full name Sadie or is Sadie short for something?
Sadie Sarah is my proper name.
HH   What is your surname ... What name besides Sadie?
Sadie Jewkes, but just call me Sadie.
HH   And you are in bed, you are not very well.
Sadie Something wrong with the milk, you see.
HH   Do you know what town you live in?
Sadie In the Lynn.
HH   Is that King's Lynn?
Sadie Yes.
HH   Do you know what year it is?
Sadie It is 1880.
HH   It's 1880. What year were you born, do you know?
Sadie (*no reply*)
HH   It is 1880, how do you know that?
Sadie ... the almanac in my diary.
HH   Do you know who rules over the land? ... (*long pause*)
       ... It doesn't matter. Do you go to school, Sadie?
Sadie I have been to school. It wasn't very good. My mama
       took me away.
HH   Do you know what time of year it is?
Sadie Nearly summer.
HH   Are you happy or sad, Sadie?
Sadie Happy.
HH   Where is your father?
Sadie He is away at sea. He is going to India.

HH   Where is your mother?

Sadie   She is in the parlour.

HH   Now time is passing ... You are growing older ... Now
        you are fifteen years old, Sadie. Where are you?

Sadie   Mama is dead ... when I was ten.

HH   And where is your father now ...?

Sadie   He is here. He is not here at the moment.

HH   He is home from the sea? Was he a ship's captain?

Sadie   Yes ... He has lots of ships.

HH   What was the ship of the last voyage he went on?

Sadie   The Omega. That is the biggest.

HH   Can you give me the name of any other ships he was
        captain of ...?

Sadie   He has a boat called the Westerly Wind.

HH   That is just a small boat, is it?

Sadie   Yes. When I was a little girl, a boy used to pretend that I
        was the captain.

HH   Does your father still go out to sea or not?

Sadie   No. He stays at home now ... He has lots of friends in
        the village.

HH   Does he do any sort of work?

Sadie   He goes to the corn exchange ... He does something,
        but I am not sure.

HH   What is the name of your house, does it have a name or
        number?

Sadie   Everyone calls it the captain's house. It has a name, but I
        can't remember it.

HH   Can you not see it written anywhere? Does it stand by
        itself?

Sadie   No.

HH   There are other houses nearby, on a road?

Sadie   Yes.

HH   What is the name of the road?

Sadie   I can't remember.

HH   Do you know the name of the rulers in England ... who
        rules the land?

Sadie   It is Queen Victoria.

(*This is correct, but of course a fairly commonly known fact.*)

HH   Have you ever seen the Queen?

Sadie   Yes, I think I have.
HH   What day is market day in King's Lynn? What day of
        the week?
Sadie   I go to market.
HH   Yes, but what day is market day; what day of the week?
Sadie   Tuesdays and Saturdays.
(She has got both days right out of a possible fifteen permutations
for the period we are speaking of, and of course correctly gave two
days where I asked her only in the singular.)
HH   Do you know the name of your doctor?
Sadie   That is Papa's friend ... Dr Thomas.
HH   Is there a squire who lives in King's Lynn ... or a mayor?
Sadie   There is a mayor.
HH   Do you know the name of the mayor? ... *(pause)* ... Do
        you know the name of the local vicar, do you go to
        church?
Sadie   We are very wicked. We don't go to church.
HH   Do you know the vicar's name?
Sadie   At St Nicholas'? *(pause)*
HH   You don't know?
Sadie   It is a pretty church.
HH   Have you ever been there?
Sadie   Oh, yes.
HH   Does anyone else live in the house besides your father
        and yourself?
Sadie   The maid ... and the cat.
HH   What do you call the cat?
Sadie   Jenkins.
HH   Are you happy or sad?
Sadie   I am sad ... I feel lonely ... I do have friends but I miss
        my Ma.
HH   Do you have any boyfriends?
Sadie   No.
HH   And you live with your father and the maid and Jenkins
        the cat in the 'captain's house'. Have you remembered
        the name?
Sadie   The West House.
HH   Now time is passing ... You are twenty ... you are
        grown up ... a woman now.

Sadie   I have got a new dress ... grey ... near the ankle. Not right down. It is very nice ... silk ... with buttons.

HH   Is your father well?

Sadie   Getting old.

HH   Still able to get about, is he?

Sadie   Yes ... I am very happy ... I am going to be married ... my lovely John ... White.

HH   Do you have an engagement ring? What is it like? Does it have diamonds?

Sadie   Rubies ... White, red, white, red.

HH   What is John's profession?

Sadie   He manages an estate ... his father's ... I think he's dead, his father.

HH   Time is passing ... you are twenty-one years old now. Have you married?

Sadie   Yes ... St Nicholas' Church ... lovely dress with roses, silk, pink.

HH   So now you are Sarah White now?

Sadie   Yes, I can't get used to that ... John is very handsome ... I love him dearly.

HH   How long have you been married?

Sadie   June 2nd, 1892. Thursday, lovely Thursday.

(*Sure enough, 2nd June that year works out to have been a Thursday.*)

HH   Now time is passing ... weeks ... months are slipping by ...

Sadie   (*interrupting*) Ooh, my eyes, I hit a branch.

HH   Were you riding?

Sadie   Yes ... It hurts so much ... some days ago. I can't move my back.

      (*She becomes very upset*) Oh, John ... I am going to die ... I don't want to die.

HH   Has the doctor been to see you? What has the doctor said?

Sadie   They are getting one from London ... Oh, I am going to die (*crying*).

HH   Time is passing ... the weeks are passing ... are you still alive?

Sadie   No.

HH   You died, Sadie? Were you still twenty-one when you
      died? Where did they bury you? Where were you buried
      when you died?
Sadie In the same place. All the same people were there.
HH   You mean in the same church ... St Nicholas' Church?
Sadie Yes. So much joy then so much sadness ...

At this point, Sadie was eased forward through the limbo until she
reached her present day persona of Tina again and my volunteer
could be restored to full consciousness and the interview ended.

In most regressions I have carried out, the subjects have shown
great emotional expression in the tone and manner of their voice
during the interviews. But none of those had quite the grasp that
Tina and her past lives showed of giving those emotions a
foundation in words. Where the tape recordings of the interview
often abound with expressive colour, Tina, or should I say Sadie,
Mary and Lucy Ann, had a knack of expressing their feelings in a
way that carries easily through to the written word. This is again
evident in her first life. Mary Kaye, later Mary Morrison, was
born in 1687. We join her as she is working in the dairy of a large
house in the Gloucester area at the age of ten. But her life takes
many turns through wealth, poverty and disease before her death
in 1717. This interview is particularly interesting for a number of
reasons. Firstly, notice how she fails to react to a couple of my
questions. She shows little reaction to the word vicar. With
hindsight, that is hardly surprising, as the equivalent man of the
church was known in those times as a rector.

The second point Mary illustrates is another of the many
curious facts that have been pieced together about the
phenomenon as a whole. How much of the past memory can be
coaxed into the present? Is it just the words and their emotional
tie-ups that are experienced as the subjects are treated to this life
replay? Or do images from the other senses also float to the
surface? The answer to the latter question, it seems, is yes. We
have known for some time that the present day subject can recall
the incidents they have relived under regression. Indeed, some
contempory hypnotherapists believe the return of these memories
to the conscious mind can be as useful in overcoming
psychological problems as the more conventional therapy of

restoring lost memories of childhood. And when seventeenth century Mary returned to her present life as Tina, she had another gift for us as well as her excellent interview. Tina asked for a pencil and paper and, after a few seconds began drawing a house. 'This,' she said, 'is where Mary lived.' So, as well as giving us an interview rich in checkable facts, she had added the medium of sight to these cameos of the past.

In the transcript which follows, as in all the others in the book, I have cut out only those questions and answers which are uninformative or repetitive, or the many short questions which are obvious by their answer. Nothing at all has been altered or added.

She begins by telling us she is Mary Kaye, aged ten, and at the moment is churning butter in the dairy at 'the Manor' in or near Gloucester:

HH   Can you remember the name of the squire you work for?

Mary Squire? ... He is a lord.

HH   Lord? Lord who? Can you remember his name?

Mary I cannot remember. I have never seen him.

HH   Do you live at the manor house?

Mary Yes.

HH   Does it stand alone in the country, near the town of Gloucester?

Mary It is not Gloucester. It is Worcester.

HH   Where do your parents live?

Mary It is two hours walking ... Stow.

HH   Can you read or write?

Mary I can write my name. K-A-Y-E.

HH   And your father?

Mary He is a shepherd.

HH   And your mother ...

Mary She looks after the children ... five ... I am the eldest.

HH   Time is passing ... You are growing up ... You are fifteen years old now. Tell me what is happening to you. Where are you now?

Mary In a house ... my father's house.

HH   At Stow-on-the-Wold. Are you on holiday?

(No reaction to the full name Stow-on-the-Wold. Despite several

*references from me, she goes on calling it simply Stow. I later
learned the other embellishments were not added until much more
recently.*)

Mary   Holiday! Someone has to look after the children.

HH   Is your mother ill?

Mary   She is confined (*a term less common nowadays for the latter stages of pregnancy*) ... more mouths to feed.

HH   And they have given you permission to come home to look after the children?

Mary   Home from where?

HH   You are not at the manor house? You do not work there now?

Mary   No ... They said I had to go ... The housekeeper, Mrs Burnett ... she doesn't like me ... said I didn't care about my work ... said 'go' ... a long time ago.

HH   And you haven't found work since? Just live with your parents?

Mary   Yes, look at me.

HH   What about you?

Mary   Dressed in rags (*she seems puzzled that I cannot see her*).

HH   Tell me now, the manor house, was it near to Worcester?

Mary   A long way from Worcester.

HH   Quite near to Stow?

Mary   Two hours walk from the manor house.

HH   Do you remember the name of the lord?

Mary   Sir.

HH   Sir what? What is his name? Can you write his name?

Mary   I cannot write ... I cannot remember ... I never saw him.

HII   Do you know what year it is, Mary?

Mary   It is 17 ... 1702.

HH   So you would be born fifteen years ago, which would be 1687?

Mary   (*laughing*) I cannot count.

HH   Has the baby arrived yet?

Mary   No.

HH   Are you going to help deliver the baby?

Mary   No.

HH   Will it be a midwife?

Mary   Yes (*she begins to show some expression of disapproval*).
HH   What are you doing?
Mary   She is always drunk ... Look at her ... dirty woman.
HH   Tell me what is happening, you are fifteen years old.
Mary   I am sick of looking like this ... rags ... black dress ... It
       is the only dress I have got.
HH   Is your house actually in Stow?
Mary   Near the market place.
HH   And your father is a shepherd?
Mary   He used to be a shepherd ... He is always drunk now ! ...
       there is no money (*laughing*) ... I have to help to get the
       money ... any way I can ... picking potatoes.
HH   Are any of the other children able to earn money?
Mary   Yes ... James ... carries the wool ... carried it for the
       master ... to the cart.
HH   To the market?
Mary   No, it is taken to town.
HH   Do you know the name of the vicar?
Mary   The vicar?
HH   The man at the church?
Mary   He is a gentleman ... he has no time for us ... I have seen
       him ... he has silver hair.
HH   Is there a doctor in Stow?
Mary   No doctor for the likes of us.
HH   Does anyone else earn money besides you and James?
Mary   Sometimes father ... He works on the land ... at harvest
       ... There is more money at harvest ... I work for a
       woman at the Inn ... God, I did everything ... the filthy
       place.
HH   Did you have to clean and cook?
Mary   Yes, and move the barrels ... She told me to get out
       (*laughing*) ... because the man had his eye on me ... I
       didn't care ... He is a horrible man ... 'Get out,' she
       screamed at me, 'Get out and don't come back' ... I just
       laughed at her.
HH   Time is passing again, Mary, you are twenty years old
       ... what is happening to you now ... Where are you
       now, Mary?
Mary   In bed ... with child.

HH   Have you married?

Mary   Yes ... he is a merchant ... Thomas, ... Tom ... Tom
        Morrison.

HH   So your name in now Mary Morrison, right?

Mary   It should have been Mary Wooler ... he went away ...
        William Wooler.

HH   Were you in love with him?

Mary   Yes.

HH   Are you in love with Tom?

Mary   No.

HH   Why did you marry him?

Mary   He is a merchant.

HH   Who made the match?

Mary   I don't know what you mean. He is a merchant.

HH   You married him because he was rich. Is he in love with
        you?

Mary   He is not a man who cares about things like that ... I
        have got the house ... I have got a bed ... It is carved.

HH   And now you are in the bed with child. When is the
        baby due?

Mary   I don't know ... in a few weeks ... I feel so ill.

HH   Weeks have gone by ... a week ... and now another ...
        Are you still in bed?

Mary   No (*sighs deeply*) ... a pain ... He should have come by
        now.

HH   What does the doctor say?

Mary   He is worried.
        (*on request, she points to the centre of pain* – in her chest.)

HH   Where is the house you live in with Tom in Stow?

Mary   Sheep Street ... no name on the door ... Everyone
        knows it's Tom Morrison's.

HH   What kind of merchant is he? What does he deal in?

Mary   Wool.

(*The emphasis on wool and its significance in the life of Stow is
certainly accurate. Records show that by 1660 dealing in sheep and
wool was the town's main trade, and by the following century more
than 20,000 sheep are said to have been sold at each fair. There is a
Sheep Street still in existence in the town and it dates back to at least
the period of this interview.*)

HH   Now time is passing. What is happening? Have you had
      the baby?
Mary The baby is dead ... no more ... no more babies ...
      There cannot be any more ... It was all for nothing.
HH   Time is passing again ... You are twenty-five years old.
      ... Where are you now?
Mary I am still in the same (*stops as if distracted*) oh dear ...
      There is something wrong ... I don't know ... There is
      a struggle ... It is the master and the men and, oh dear,
      the women ... in the street.

*(She becomes agitated, so I ask her by way of distracting, the name
of the present king. She answers Queen Anne, which is correct. This
tactic has been occasionally necessary with the subjects and explains
why I often abandon or postpone some potentially interesting lines
of questioning.)*

HH   And what is happening outside?
Mary There is someone and he has stolen something. He is
      poaching and they are going to get him ... It is not fair,
      because he was so hungry ... They say he is going to
      hang ... Oh God.
HH   They are going to hang him? Where will they hang him?
Mary At the cross ... just outside Stow ... there is a stone
      cross.

*(The next passage is interesting as a counterargument to one theory
that the scenes in regression depend on leading questions. Despite
my confusion about the town's hierarchy, Mary leads me through
and parries each question with quick consistency.)*

HH   Who will decide what? Will it be the squire who decides
      or the lord of the manor?
Mary It is not the squire; it is the magistrate.
HH   What is his name?
Mary The magistrate?
HH   The squire is the magistrate?
Mary Rawlings.
HH   Squire Rawlings? Where does he live, in Stow?
Mary I cannot remember where he lives.
HH   Who, the squire? Doesn't he live at the manor?
Mary No, the magistrate.
HH   Isn't the magistrate the squire?

Mary   No.

HH   Can you remember the name of the lord of the manor
       where you worked when you were a girl?

Mary   It begins with T ... Trevelyan ... Sir Charles Trevelyan.

HH   And what is the name of the man at the church with
       silver hair?

Mary   Carter ... I cannot remember the church.

*(At this point I advanced her to thirty years from her birth, but she
leads me to believe she died in the meantime, so we return, this time
four years to when she was twenty-six. She tells me she is tired
because she is suffering from a fever and has spots.)*

HH   What kind of spots?

Mary   Red spots ... lips are swollen ... The doctor won't come
       ... He is too afraid ... the fever ... Thomas is dead ...
       died first ... I nursed him ... There is a lot of talk about
       it ... Nobody dare say what they really think ... too
       afraid ... Oh, God, there is a smell ... Nobody will come
       ... The girl has gone home *(a servant)* ... Nobody dare.

*(The symptoms fit closely to those of smallpox, and local records
show that there were major outbreaks of the disease in the Stow area
as often as 1644, 1646, 1758, 1831, 1833 and 1852. Although, by
Mary's reckoning, the year is now 1713, we were at first content with
a near miss. But then a specialist local historian discovered records
of an unusually high number of deaths in Stow that year. The cause is
not named, but it seems to have taken several members of each
afflicted family at a time, which points, very strongly, to some kind
of epidemic.*

*Mary's expression of shame and embarrassment about her disease
tallies closely with the reason why some outbreaks never reached the
record books – and why some of those which did were not named.
Such was the social disgrace associated with smallpox, that often
people would try to pretend that it had not struck at all. In the 1758
Stow outbreak, churchwardens afterwards denied its existence. The
principal cause of the shame is thought to have been the extremely
unpleasant symptoms.*

*Smallpox, assuming that is what she describes, is usually fatal,
though it is not unknown for someone to survive it. When I advance
Mary another year, I discover that she has been one of those people.
She has held onto her life ... but what a life it is now.)*

Mary I have recovered but look at me ... I have got the scars.
HH   Did they ever find out what kind of fever it was? Was it smallpox?
Mary Yes.
HH   What happened to Thomas?
Mary He left me with nothing ... I don't know where the money has gone ... I have sold some of the furniture ... Where can I go? ... I never leave this house ... except at dusk ... to see someone ... the old woman ... She gives me things ... herbs ... I am so tired.
HH   Now a year has passed and you are twenty-nine years old ... Are you still alive?
Mary Yes. There is no money at all ... I can hardly get out of the chair ... Starving ... There is no furniture left, hardly ... Nobody wants this furniture now ... it is so old.

(*I advance Mary another year to a time very shortly after her death and, curiously, she is out of her body but physically very close to it, apparently concerned that no one has discovered it. It is interesting also that, when she leaves this state into the 'limbo' state, she herself announces that she is moving forward.*)

Mary She is still there ... She is ... in the chair ...
HH   Your body? Is it dead?
Mary Yes.
HH   You have left the body. Has anyone found her yet?
Mary No.
HH   How long ago did she die?
Mary Hours.
HH   When did you leave her body?
Mary Don't know. Moving forward.

Mary's body, along with her name and environment, is left behind now and this indeterminate essence of memory alone moves forward until we reach its next apparent exploration in earthbound form. This time – Tina's second life, chronologically – we meet Lucy-Anne Partridge, a spinster who began her generous span of sixty-two years exactly the same number of years since the previous death she told us of in 1717. In Anne, we meet a girl plagued throughout her life with apparently agonising headaches which she describes in childhood as earache. Her frequent hand gestures during this interview gave me some idea of the intensity of pain. She seemed to use her hands a lot during her regression as Anne, each time acting out in mime whatever action she was performing at that time.

She tells us at ten years old that she is in bed with a bandage around her head for earache. Two years later in her life, we find she lives in Plymouth; her mother's name is Emily. Her house is in a curved road simply called The Crescent. She used to have a tutor, but now she is taught by her mother. She lives in the reign of King George but does not know which one, and her father is in the Army.

Anne He is very important ... wears red.

HH   And what sort of dress do you wear?

Anne Long white chiffon ... feels nice. Very soft and nice to touch ... white ... blue underneath.

(*Taken to the age of fifteen, she can now give her full address as Sixteen The Crescent and at the moment the month is November.*)

Anne There is something wrong ... Everybody is crying.

HH   Do you have any brothers or sisters?

Anne Yes, two sisters.

HH   Do you know what rank your father holds in the Army?

Anne Captain ... He is not in the Army now ... He has left the Army ... we have to leave ... There is no money.

HH   Is your father not there, someone taken him away?

Anne Yes, yesterday or today. I can't remember ... they were not nice.

HH   Were they in uniform?

Anne No ... mother says we must pack.

(*One year forward again and now the family live in rooms somewhere near the sea. She does not think much of the place and says the woman who owns it is always staring. Father is still away, but Anne does not know where. She refers again to 'one of my headaches', suggesting that they happen often. No one works, the family has no money. Anne spends her days at home looking after her mother. She begins to make some apparently functional movement with her hands.*)

HH   What are doing with your hands?

Anne I am just straightening the cloth ... on the table ... going to write a letter ... to father.

(*He is in prison but she does not know why, or in which prison he is held. It was not in the interview, but during cataloguing by G.V.I. that we learned the charge was embezzlement. If she writes the letter, she says, her mother will see it gets to him. We join her again at the age of eighteen.*)

Anne Just getting dressed ... going out.

HH   Are you going to meet someone?

Anne Yes.

HH   Your young man?

Anne No ... I don't know who I will meet till I get there ... It is
       a ball ... with my friend ... Her name is Lucinda.

(*Twenty-three years old now and she is outside somewhere, near the stables. Father is now dead. He came home from prison and mother said he was a broken man. They are living with an aunt in a big house. She is to marry a man named Robert but gives no reply as to his surname. Again she begins to move her hands, saying she is stroking a horse. As I take her to thirty years old she grasps her head in pain, so we back-track to twenty-eight. We learn little here except that the house is called the Grey House, she is not keen on her aunt and her sister Becky is married. But as for her own love life, Robert has left her and she feels she is now too old to have much hope of ever marrying. Now, she is thirty-three.*)

Anne Becky is here today ... She has two children.

HH   What happened to your other sister?

Anne ... She didn't marry ... She died when she was a little
       girl.

HH   ... Why did she die? (*no answer*) ... How do you spend
       your time at the Grey House, with the horses?

Anne Yes. I like horses ... I like to draw.

(*Forty years old now, still at the Grey House, though alone, as both mother and aunt are dead.*)

HH   Is it your house now? Are you the mistress?

Anne No, Becky is here ... It is Becky's and my house ... and
       the children.

HH   Her children and her husband? What is he called?

Anne I don't like him ... He is not a nice man.

HH   Does Becky like him?

Anne I suppose so. She has got very fat.

HH   Are you in good health?

Anne Except for my headaches.
(*Fifty now. Things still the same. Still sharing the house with Becky.*)
Anne She is a nuisance ... She wants to change everything.
HH   Do you quarrel?
Anne Yes.
HH   What about – the children?
Anne John is away at school. The girl is still here.
HH   How do you spend your time – riding and painting?
Anne Too old to ride ... I cannot see very well.
(*Fifty-five now. Still at the Grey House with Becky.*)
Anne Becky! She is so fat ... She dresses like a young girl ...
      Becky is ten years younger than me.
(*At sixty-two her feelings seem to harden even more.*)
Anne She wants me dead ... Then she can own the house.
HH   Are you in good health?
Anne No.
(*I try to take her to a later time but she argues that she does not want
to go. Each time I say sixty-five, she repeats sixty-two.*)
HH   Don't you want to be sixty-five?
Anne No ... it's horrible ... cannot move.
HH   Are you alive or dead, Anne?
Anne I don't know. I can see her.
(*Here again, she seems in close proximity to her dead body. But here
is a twist. Her tale take a macabre turn as, after identifying the
church as St Michael's, she describes her own burial.*)
HH   Can you see anything?
Anne Something large.
HH   Is it a person or a thing?
Anne I don't know ... Get it away! ... It is the earth coming
      down on top of me ... horrid ... in the ground ... It is all
      so heavy ... Cannot get out ... Cannot get away ...

At this stage she became more agitated with her conscious
experience of the horror of interment and I moved her back to the
present after briefly checking that there were no lives that the
cataloguing may have missed. As usual, the cataloguing showed
itself to be accurate, and she slipped through Sadie back into Tina
and the end of the interview.

4
Hazel – Beauty Through the Eyes of Death

This book is written without preconceived conclusions. The whole purpose of seeking historical backing for these newly illuminated pockets of the past is, at best, to narrow down the field of possibilities. That is to say, stack up enough positive findings from the archives and you have, at least in theory, proven that these enigmatic interviews are renderings of some real event or person from the past.

Or, of course, you could begin the other way round. You could start with a belief, and then proceed only down those paths which you believe will nourish that preconception. But in exploring this particular branch of the unknown we are fumbling in the dark. And to select only material that supports a preconception would impede our exploration further. The central point of that preconception could be any one of many current theories. Any time I have mentioned this project to anyone, they all automatically jump to the same conclusion – that I must be a believer in reincarnation. They are all led, for some reason, to think that a pre-packed belief in something of that ilk could be my only motivation for mounting this project in the first place. But in fact the exact opposite is true. I have deliberately fought off any tendency to believe in any one of the theories more than the others. My only belief is in the absolute importance of the lack of a specific belief. To approach the subject with anything less than an open mind would instantly weigh the research with intolerable limitations, and the results would just as instantly alienate themselves from anyone holding anything but the same belief. I learnt this to my cost at a very early stage in the historical checking. There is no quicker way to lose the invaluable assistance of any parish vicar than to let slip the word 'reincarnation'.

If I had begun with any such belief, then the next subject and her 'family' of four lives would probably never have seen the light of day. As well as being for the most part uninteresting, the lives of Hazel are the hardest knock that could be dealt to any preconception. They show a startling amount of negative validation, even – and this is puzzling – to the extent of shunning publicly available information in favour of flimsy make believe. In her earliest life, she insists that she lives in two apparently non-existent villages near Weybridge, Surrey, when surely a playful unconscious would simple settle its fantasy on the town itself?

But there was an even greater disappointment to be found in her latest life. At first it held out a great deal of hope, for it was the most recent of all the crop of lives I have delved in, and thus it had the greatest potential for validation. Her house not only still exists but was allegedly occupied by the 'life' well within this century and therefore in easy reach of electoral registers. But my elation was short lived when I discovered that no one of her name, or any even vaguely similar name, had lived in that house or anywhere near at the time in question.

Nonetheless, I feel honour bound to give the bad news as well as the good so here, warts and all (may she forgive the metaphor) is Hazel, a thirty-eight year old health visitor and mother of three who begins her interview in the most recent life, and says she is Peggy.

Peggy (Margaret) Brown says she is ten years old in 1912 and lives in Peckham Rye, London. The daughter of a farrier, she seems not to know her address at that age but then says at fifteen that they live at number eight, Ondine Road. This road did exist and indeed still does, in SE15 near Peckham Rye Common.

She insists at the age of fifteen firstly that the year is 1919 and then that the country is at war. If the year were correct, this would clearly be a fundamental mistake. But if someone born in 1902 is fifteen years old, then the year must be 1917, not 1919. This could be a curious mistake for anyone who knows of the 1914–1918 War from hearsay, as the dates are as deeply ingrained in most minds almost as 1066. But would not someone drawing from living memory relate more to her own age at a certain time than the year on the calendar? However, this little teaser is Peggy's only offering which rises above humdrum, except perhaps for odd geometric visions after death, so I shall be brief in relating the interview. As we join her, she is still fifteen years old.

HH   Have you any brothers or sisters?
Peggy   Yes.
HH   Are they older than you?
Peggy   Bertie is.
HH   Has he gone to war?
Peggy   Yes.
HH   Where is he now?
Peggy   Don't know.

*(Twenty years old now, and she is walking in the neighbourhood
to meet someone)*

Peggy   A young man ... Jack.
HH   What is his other name?
Peggy   Don't know.

*(Taken to twenty-five years old, she gives no reaction to questioning
until asked if she is still alive.)*

Peggy   I don't think so.
HH   What are you feeling?
Peggy   Circles ... black ones getting smaller and coming in ...
        I think I may not be alive.

*(I take her back to twenty, then check life at yearly intervals, and
again we reach twenty-five, presumably earlier in the year.*

HH   Are you no longer alive now? What caused your death?
Peggy   (*puzzled*) I am not dead ...
HH   Are you ill?
Peggy   Yes ... headaches ... Cannot see ... Cannot open my
        eyes ... I am in the hospital.
HH   Is your name still Margaret Brown?
Peggy   No, Margaret Swales ... about four years ... Jack.
HH   What does the doctor say is the matter?
Peggy   They never tell me.
HH   Another month has passed. Are you still alive?
Peggy   No.
HH   What do you mean?
Peggy   Black circles.
HH   What do you feel?
Peggy   Purple circles.
HH   Can you feel anything?
Peggy   No.
HH   Can you remember where they buried your body?

Peggy   Yes. St Michael's.
HH   Is that in Peckham?
Peggy   Yes.

Poor Hazel seems to have suffered the same total lack of excitement in the next life as well. In fact one could say that being dead held a great deal more for the fishwife named Mary Gates than being alive ever did. For after her humdrum existence was ended by hypothermia around 1852, she was surrounded by a most beautiful vision – a vision which must be the most powerful symbol of peace to anyone whose livelihood is eked from the sea. Accompanied by a great feeling of peace, Mary floated onwards through her inter-life limbo to the sight of the sun over the water. But, on a less aesthetic level, she does have one offering of value to anyone believing that the subject's suggestibility may have some part in the phenomenon. See how she reacts when I try to assert what I think her date of birth should be:

HH   How old are you?
Mary   Fifteen.
HH   What year is it?
Mary   1810
HH   So you must have been born in 1795.
Mary   No.
HH   If you are fifteen – the year is 1810 now – so you would
         be born in 1795. If you take fifteen away from 1810,
         what year does that make it?
Mary   1795.
HH   Is that the year you were born?
Mary   1796.

(She continues to tell us that she lives in Dover and her father is a fish porter or something similar. She marries James Parker at the age of nineteen and they have three children. She loses her husband through chest trouble in a bad winter and her son is lost at sea. We take it up again when she is fifty, soon after these tragedies.)

HH   What does Robert (*another son*) do? Is he a sailor as well?
Mary   He is a carpenter.
HH   Were you upset when James died?
Mary   Yes, he was a good lad.
HH   Time is passing now. You are sixty years old . . . Are you
         still living in Dover?

Mary   No.
HH   Where are you living now?
Mary   Nowhere.
(*She says she died at fifty-six years old.*)
HH   What did you die of?
Mary   Cold, very cold.
HH   Did they bury you in the churchyard?
Mary   Next to James ... St Bartholemew's and All Angels.
HH   What do you feel?
Mary   I see the sun shining on the water.
HH   And you have been dead for about three or four years?
Mary   Yes.
HH   What do you feel?
Mary   Peaceful.

The normal attempts were made to find validation for this life but nothing could be found that could confirm that Mary Gates either did or did not exist.

But at least things are looking up a little for modern-day Hazel. In her next life back – the second chronologically – she becomes Katie Blackthorne, daughter of the Mayor of Chichester and is, at least at the age of ten, a happy child. I ask her at fifteen if she is able to write.

Katie   Yes.
HH   What would you write if you had to put the date on the top of a letter?
Katie   The fourteenth February.
HH   What year?
Katie   1510.
HH   And you live in the mayor's house. Do you know the name of the road?
Katie   It is in the square – just the square.
HH   Is it a nice house? Does it have a lot of rooms?
Katie   Oh, yes ... quite a lot.
HH   When your father was not Mayor of Chichester, what was his occupation? How did he make his living?
Katie   He was a corn merchant.
HH   Do you know the name of the King?
Katie   Henry.

HH   Which of the Henries? Henry who?

Katie   Henry VII.

(*The reign of Henry VII ended in 1509 and Henry VIII succeeded to the Throne.*)

HH   Do you go to school or do you have a tutor?

Katie   No, I have a tutor.

HH   What day of the week is market day in Chichester?

Katie   On Thursday.

HH   What sort of clothes do you wear, skirts or dresses?

Katie   Dresses.

HH   Long dresses?

Katie   (*a little shocked*) Of course, long dresses.

HH   Do they have belts or are they just made tight?

Katie   Sashes ... my best one has.

HH   What sort of food do you have at home?

Katie   Just ordinary food, beef, fowl.

(*The preference for meat in Tudor times is legendary. It occurred to such an extent that wealthy people were known to suffer from vitamin deficiencies through low intake of vegetables. These carried the social stigma of being more suited to the poor.*)

HH   How much would a fowl cost in the market?

Katie   I don't know. I don't shop.

HH   Now time is passing ... You are twenty years old ...
        What is happening now?

Katie   I am waiting for somebody to come and see me ... Steven.

HH   What is Steven's other name?

Katie   It isn't Steven, it's Silas.

HH   Why did you say Steven?

Katie   Because I don't like Silas.

HH   What is his other name?

Katie   Oakes.

HH   Silas Oakes?

Katie   It's stupid.

HH   Are you still in the mayor's house?

Katie   We are still in the same house in the square.

(*She later explains that her father is no longer mayor; one assumes their home loses its title as well. When I tried to check the past mayors of the town, via a friend who lives locally, she could find several up to 1506 and after 1512, but a curious gap where the enigmatic Mr Blackthorne should have occurred.*)

  HH   How do you spend your time, Katie?

Katie I sew – also embroider.

HH   Has your father gone back to being a corn merchant?

Katie Yes.

HH   How long was he mayor?

Katie Four years.

HH   What else do you do?

Katie I play the harpsichord.

HH   Have you had any new clothes lately?

Katie Yes, a green velvet gown.

HH   Does it come right down to the floor?

Katie It does.

(*Once again she seems a little affronted at my hint of doubt on the question of dress length. This is not very difficult to understand if you consider that during such periods women were so fully covered that anything less would be thought indecent.*)

HH   Now time is passing again … You are twenty-five years old … What is happening now … Did you marry Steven?

Katie No … I don't know why … Richard … Mortimer.

HH   Do you live with Richard Mortimer?

Katie Yes … and Agnes … my servant … Florence Street. Forty-one, Florence Street.

(*There is a Florence Road in the city to this day, but apparently no Florence Street.*)

HH   What does Richard do for a living?

Katie He helps his father … Peter Mortimer … he sells cloth.

(*Thirty-five now and the mother of four. Her father-in-law has died.*)

Katie We have a fine house now … it is just outside the town … you go out of the west side of the town and there is a track. You go down the track and it is on the right hand side … you will see it; it's the only one there … Burton House.

(*Now to fifty years old and something is disturbing her.*)

Katie Cannot see.

HH   Are you blind?

Katie Yes.

HH   Do you still live with Richard?

Katie No, he is dead . . . just the servants . . . I went blind slowly
       and now I cannot see at all . . . about four years.
*(But her blindness ends with her death, it seems, and once again
Hazel in limbo reports some visual experience as she tells us of
Katie's death at fifty-seven.)*
HH   What did you die of?
Katie Just old age . . . no pain.
HH   Where did they bury your body?
Katie In Chichester . . . St Mary's.
HH   Now you are dead, can you see anything?
Katie Blue.
HH   Can you feel anything?
Katie Happy.

As I said much earlier, in the search to explain the source of the whole past life regression phenomenon, we are perhaps missing something by blaming it all on a single cause. You yourself may say it is definitely reincarnation or ancestral memory or even simply imagination. But it seems more and more likely that what we are looking at is a hybrid of two of the possibilities. As to the principal source the answer is still as thickly veiled in mystery as ever. But there can be little doubt that secondary source is fantasy. But what kind of fantasy? Can there possibly be any conscious deception? The answer to that is a simple 'no'. In the very deep trance state needed to probe these historical times, it is unlikely that the conscious mind in its greatly reduced sense of awareness could conjure up any such prolonged fantasies.

The subject is so totally relaxed that even the task of speaking seems to demand supreme effort. One can only lie if one is forming one's thoughts. But in the fully regressed subject the thoughts simply fall out of the mind unaided. So what about laying the blame on the unconscious mind for all this embroidery of fact? That is the only answer left, but there is one detail yet to be considered – when does this apparently pointless act of playwriting go on? One thing is sure – the mind does not wait to be asked a question before it composes the fantasy parts of the answer. Every reply comes not only almost instantly but also ready tailored to fit the entire plot around it.

So, the most logical conclusion seems to be this: in every one of us there sits a little bookshelf of maybe four or five plays, each one of the 'dramatised true story' type. But in the overwhelming majority of cases the books will lay undisturbed throughout the owner's entire life – until that life itself simply becomes yet another book to put at the end of the shelf that has the thinnest layer of dust.

What I am leading up to, taking into account the balance of fantasy and proveable fact in each life interviewed, is my belief that we should not be tempted to dismiss any of our characters from the past simply because more of what they say defies validation. Some do tend to spike their factual information with far more of the daydream ingredient than others. And just one such is Frances Moore, the earliest person recorded for Hazel.

Frances brings us great chunks of history which defy any attempt at validation despite what was probably the most thorough search of the whole project. She speaks of great monetary wealth and property, which, if it were factual, must have left a significant mark on the records of the day. But no. Frances, her money, land and homes seem to have vaporised as soon as her regression interview ended, and if these things ever did exist they have been magnificently camouflaged. Though why, when even the conscious mind carries its own gazetteer of accurate place names by the thousand, the unconscious should feel the need to spice its tales with fantasy ones remains beyond even my comprehension.

She begins in 1192 by telling us she lives in the village of Bridlethorpe, which we conclude by her later life is supposed to be in Surrey. Neither modern maps nor the *Domesday Book*, in either text or map, show any trace of such a place.

Then she says the nearest town to hold a market is Weybridge, and that market is on a Friday. We do not know the truth of the Friday market, but can guess at its unlikelihood by the fact that only forty-seven years later the formal granting of a weekly market was given to Geoffrey De Lucy – for a Tuesday.

HH Do you know who rules the land?
Frances King John.
(*She tells us this in 1196, three years before John came to the Throne.*)
HH And what does your father do?
Frances He travels quite often ... He jurisdicts (!) ... travels

round the villages and holds court ... He is a
magistrate.

*(This post was usually held by earls at that time but there is no record
of an earl of that name in any of the contemporary records.)*

HH   Do you have a doctor in the village who visits?

Frances Yes ... Dr Frankish.

(Once again, no trace.)

HH   Do you remember the name of the Church where you
go?

Frances It is the Church of the Martyrs.

*(She also mentions this later as the place where she is married, but it
is not recorded in* English Historical Document.*)*

Later she says she has now married the 'moderately wealthy'
Richard Beaufort and is living in Raisebek, ten miles from
Weybridge. But the first historical mention of the surname does
not come until 200 years later, and once again neither text nor
map of the *Domesday Book* can shed any light on Raisebek. The
odd spelling, incidentally, is hers, as she very carefully spelled it
out for me.

But then comes a fairly accurate piece of reportage, albeit a bit
jumbled:

Frances There is trouble ... fighting ... My husband and the
servants fighting with the people who want to take
away our land ... the King's soldiers.

*(Then five years later she says they managed to get some of their
land back. According to* The Life and Times of King John *by
Maurice Ashley, there was widespread fighting in the exact year she
names – 1216 – but Surrey was among the King's allies. And by the
time Surrey had joined the rebels in supporting the invasion of Louis
of France, John would be far too occupied defending his country to
be thinking of petty confiscations.)*

Frances's mode of burial is at least interesting, though again
without a shred of validation. She tells us her body had to be
buried in the grounds of the Monastery of the Brothers of St Igna-
tious because 'there is dissent in the Church ... they denounced the
priest'. Whether she means a specific church or the organisation on
a wider basis is hard to tell. There were religious quarrels between
the monarchy and Rome, but they were some years earlier.

5
Rosamund

We must travel back more than two thousand years before we reach the start of the next sequence of lives. That is where we find the apparent beginning of a string of existences which connects the idyllic life of a wealthy woman of ancient Greece with a Teeside schoolteacher and mother of three.

For someone with Rosamund's background, she shows a remarkable grasp of Greek island geography when she regresses to become Andromache. She has never been to Greece, never studied its history, never taught geography; and the only point of contact she can recall is a single reading of Homer's *Odyssey* some years ago. Yet when the personality of Rosamund receded to allow Andromache to the fore, we get a very different picture. Odysseus to her becomes a point of reference on which to base the calendar (in the same way as we use the birth of Christ) and lands still traceable on the maps of today become islands to point to beyond the horizon, where relatives live and traders come and go. Of course, with such a long span in time – this is the second earliest of all the lives I have found – hopes of a full validation become rather more limited. But in something as changeless as geography, where modern maps differ so little from those of her time, she shows an accuracy which goes a long way towards making up for this. Evidence of this begins with her first interview, when the ten year old Andromache, or Andrie, as her friends call her, describes her environment for the first time:

HH   What country do you live in?
Andromache It is an island ... Zanthos.
(*There is an island which was known in those times as Zakinthos and which fits in with later descriptions.*)
HH   And what town on Zanthos do you live in?
Andromache There are no towns, only villages.
HH   What is the name of the village where you live?

Andromache Er ... K ... I'm not sure.

*(Modern maps show four villages on Zakinthos – two of them begin
with 'K'. There is Katastari to the north of the island and Keri near
the southern tip.)*

HH   Do you know to which country the island of
            Zanthos really belongs?

Andromache It is one of many islands ... just one of many
            islands.

*(The coastal waters of Greece around that area are dotted with
islands.)*

HH   And how do you spend your time, Andromache?

Andromache Well, we play a lot on the beach (*both the villages
            mentioned are coastal*) ... I sometimes help
            mother with weaving ... I look after the goats.

HH   You look after the goats? ... and sheep?

Andromache Not sheep, only goats.

HH   What do you weave?

Andromache Clothes, cloaks, wall hangings ... from goat's
            hair, and sometimes wool from another island.

HH   Do you know the name of the nearest big piece
            of land to your islands?

Andromache Pelopennesia.

*(The island which appears to have been her home is immediately
adjacent to Pelopennesia.)*

HH   And how are you dressed, Andromache?

Andromache When I am on the beach we usually take our
            clothes off, but I have got my tunic on the stones.

(To twenty years old now and it seems she has moved away to marry.)

HH   Where are you?

Andromache On the island of Ithica ... with my husband.

(Ithica is the next island but one if you travel north from Zakinthos.)

HH   How old were you when you married?

Andromache About fourteen.

HH   Have you any children?

Andromache Yes, two.

HH   How do you give a date to everything? How are
            you able to record time?

Andromache We think back to things that have happened and
            count on from them.

HH	Can you tell me of any big happenings that you date things from?
Andromache	The return of Odysseus from Ilium (*Ilium is the Greek name for Troy.*)
HH	Have you ever heard of a place called Rome?
Andromache	No.
HH	Or Greece?
Andromache	No.

(*She goes on to describe her dress as a tunic worn below the knee and held with a bronze brooch and a girdle. She says it is a twisted girdle, which gathers the tunic in pleats around the waist.*)

HH	Do you have special clothes you wear at night?
Andromache	No, we don't usually wear clothes for sleeping.
HH	What kind of bed do you sleep in?
Andromache	It is a sort of box shape in the corner of the wall … In the summer we have thin, fine woven woollen sheets. In the winter we sleep on the skins with more skins on the top … goat skins.

(*There is little of additional interest in this session. She does, however, identify one more island, Skiros, to where she says her daughter moves when she is married. Skiros does exist, but it is some distance away on the other side of the mainland. It is also interesting to hear how her remains were disposed of after her death at fifty-one years old, and also her eerie entrance into the memory of the next life.*)

HH	How did they dispose of your body?
Andromache	They burned it on the beach and put the ashes in a big earthenware urn in a cave.
HH	Are there other urns in the cave with ashes in them?
Andromache	Yes, my husband's and his ancestors'.

(*I direct her now to float forwards until she is aware of being in another body, then ask her her name.*)

| Andromache | I don't know, I only feel sort of very vaguely … No, I am not properly there yet … I feel vaguely aware of being with a lot of other people outside a house made of wood and mud and a thatched roof, but I feel like a shadow, as if I were not properly there. |

HH   Do you have a name?
Rosamund   I don't know.

Straight on now to the second interview with Andromache. This, like the other in-depth interviews, was based on questions unseen by me before the session and drawn from validation research on the first interview. I begin with a little geography test:

HH   Can you tell me the name of any of the islands near?
Andromache Samathrace.

(There are two islands of this name. One is to the west of Greece in the Mediterranean, the other to the east in the Aegean.)

HH   In what direction does it lie?
Andromache When you stand on Zanthos and look away from the way you would go towards Ithica.

(If you think that is confusing, read on.)

HH   It lies in the opposite direction to Ithica?
Andromache Well, not really. Zanthos lies in such a place that you would have to ... *(pause)* If you look in the direction of Samothrace you would have to go back along a sort of flat bit of the mainland and up to Ithica.
HH   Can you tell me ... the names of any inhabited islands ... nearest to Ithica?
Andromache Naxos ... quite near.

(There is an island of Naxos, but it is much farther round the coast to the west in the Cyclades islands.)

HH   What direction is it from Ithica?

(I should have learnt by now not to ask.)

Andromache Again, if you imagine standing looking the way I described on Zanthos, it would be to my right and slightly forward.
HH   Is there a place called Samos near to Ithica?
Andromache Yes.

(Samos is again nowhere near Ithica, but it is quite close to Naxos.)

HH   Is there a place called Cephallenia?
Andromache No.

(This is interesting. Cephallenia is not only quite large but also very close to Ithica. Her answer, even an apparently incorrect one, says a

*lot about the possibility of subjects being influenced by leading
questions. But her next answer is even more of a puzzle.)*

HH	Is there a place called Zakinthos?
Andromache	Yes.
HH	Is it an island?
Andromache	I am not sure. It is a name I have heard.

*(Zakinthos, you will recall, is the island we had interpreted to be her
home. It is of course possible that our interpretation is wrong and she
is right, but I can find no other likely island of a similar name to
Zanthos.)*

HH	Do you know the name of the person who rules over Athens?
Andromache	I believe he is called Pericles.

*(Pericles ruled the state of Athens from 461 BC to 429 BC. Now, take
note of the next answers, as she seems to contradict her lack of
knowledge later in the interview.)*

HH	Have you heard of a place called Ilium?
Andromache	Yes.
HH	Do you know if it has any other name, or is it just Ilium?
Andromache	As far as I know, it is only called Ilium.
HH	Was it recently sacked, or has it been sacked at some time in the past?
Andromache	A long, long time ago. Odysseus was there.
HH	Do you know the name of the king of Ilium now?
Andromache	I don't think there is a king of Ilium now. I think when Ilium was destroyed, it was destroyed forever.

*(Ilium, as I said earlier, was the Greek name for Troy – thus my
question about other names for it – and it was destroyed by
Odysseus early in the first millenium BC. She goes on to tell us of
places on the mainland called Mycenae, Sparta and Corinth, which
are all correct but fairly well-known anyway. Asked who rules
Sparta, she says Antonidas 'or some such name', where the ruler was
in fact Archidamus. When I ask her if she has heard of Cnossus, she
answers 'yes, that is one of the places my husband visits in Crete'.
Cnossus was indeed in Crete; on the northern coast. The following
description she gives of a ship seems to match very well those from
records of the time.)*

Andromache It has a big square sail ... not quite square ...
wider than it is tall ... just one ... Oh, I think
(*the ship*) would be about thirty paces, but I
would be guessing ... room for about twelve
rowers on each side ... a sort of cabin in the
centre and some room under the planks.

*(Her home, she continued, is made of stone from Ithica and has a
main room and a number of bedrooms. The next few minutes of the
interview are taken up with similar everyday descriptions – baking
bread, farmwork, jewellery and so on, but there is little or nothing
which could not have been guessed, so it is not a great deal of use to
us. The next significant point is her second reference to dates.)*

HH You said that you count time from the return of
Odysseus ... Can you tell me how long ago
that was?

Andromache Oh, it is very many years ago, I think ... it was
my husband's, oh, seven or eight ancestors
back.

*(This seems to be a shorter time than generally believed between the
fall of Troy and the reign of Pericles.)*

HH What do you know about the story of Odysseus?

Andromache I know he went to fight a great war in Troy ...
And it was he who invented the idea of the wooden
horse which got our people into the city.

HH Where is Troy?

Andromache Troy, I think, is Ilium ... It is usually known as
Ilium.

*(She now appears to have remembered both names despite her
inability earlier.)*

Before concluding this interview with Andromache, I asked her
to speak to me using some of her own language instead of my
usual instruction to subjects to use their modern day language and
dialect. This was the result, written phonetically, '*Lexos esuf
natulos ist za dranst int lexos tempos mark*'. She said the meaning
of this sentence was, 'the time between is too great to remember'.
Even though the Greek of that period was split into many very
strong dialects, and our knowledge of the language itself is far
from complete, there is little that can be made from Andro-

mache's statement. Experts to whom I have shown this say there are some snippets of linguistic roots from both Greek and Latin, but the sentence as a whole is quite indecipherable. This is perhaps not as disappointing as it may seem at first. It is true that it indicates almost beyond doubt that Andromache in the twentieth century knows no classical Greek. However, true cases of xenoglossy – speaking in tongues one has never learnt – are very rare, and we must bear in mind again that we are stirring memories many centuries old, or claimed to be so. Even if names and mental pictures survive well, it is possible that memories of language may fade. As Andromache herself says, the time between is too great to remember.

Rosamund has a further three lives before her present one, but despite the early start in ancient Greece there is a gap of more than two thousand years before she reappears in human form. Then, as if to make up for this, the subsequent gaps are far shorter than normal. Her second 'death' lasts only twenty-five years, her third only eight years, and then the birth of Rosamund follows her most recent death in regression by a more normal eighty one years.

Her second life, as Janousa Van Djrin, is rather confusing in a number of ways. She says that although they live in the Netherlands her father is Danish, yet their surname is clearly Dutch. There is really little of interest in the rest of her interview except for one short passage and the validation which backs it up.

HH   What kind of language do they speak in your country?
Janousa Basque.
HH   Do all the people in your land speak that language?
Janousa Just this part of it.

After the confusion over her Dutch/Danish father, I was tempted to write this off, and not even try to research the point. The idea of this Spanish-derived language being used in Holland seemed ridiculous. But why did she bother to say it was spoken only in a part of the country? I decided to check it out after all, and was very pleasantly surprised with my findings. It seems that during the period in question – around 1740 – there was quite a sizeable migration of Basques into the Netherlands. Again, the strength of such a confirmation is in its obscurity. This seems far too insignificant a fact to be mentioned in even the more advanced of school history lessons, certainly far more advanced that Rosamund ever experienced. She has no knowledge outside hypnosis of ever hearing such a thing, and no idea of any circumstances under which she may have heard but forgotten it.

It has struck me as curious and quite inexplicable that during the project, based on volunteers from the north east of England, most of the lives we turned up were based around the south and south west. Perhaps the distribution of population in the past has a great deal to do with that. But beyond that, there was another little geographic oddity which I can only put down to coincidence – the number of past lives that appear to have taken place in the area of Bath. I once saw a poster which advertised a seaside town with the catchphrase, 'there's something about us that makes you want to come back'. Perhaps the city of Bath should adopt the same slogan, but add, '… after a hundred years or so'.

Apart from the dubious honour of being one of the Bath-based lives, Rosamund's third life as Amanda Rodgers holds little of interest at all, except for a few negative validation results which I should mention in the name of impartiality – such as an untraceable vicar for a father and a claim to have read *Vanity Fair*, twenty-two years before the birth of its author – I shall pass Amanda by and move straight to Jane Williams.

It was right at the beginning of Jane's interview that I came across the puzzling street name I mentioned in the introductory chapter.

HH   What town do you live in?
Jane   (*At this point ten years old*) in London … near St Paul's.
HH   Do you know the name of the street or road?
Jane   Yes … it's Ludgate Street.

(*Even after the researcher stumbled on the name in the face of the old clock, it took quite a bit of further digging to find confirmation in more formal records. Eventually, we discovered that prior to 1865 the part of Ludgate Hill from the old Ludgate to St Paul's was known as Ludgate Street. And that is not all we found …*)

HH   Is your father alive?
Jane   Yes … he is a baker.

(*According to Johnstone's* London Directory, *around the stated year of 1815, there was a pastry cook and confectioner in Ludgate*

*Hill and another a couple of years later in Ludgate Street itself.
Neither of these shops however, bore the name Williams. But Jane
does not actually say that her father's shop had the family name,
although it would be unlikely not to. There was a trader by the name
of Williams in Ludgate Street at that time, but the* Directory *says he
was a manufacturer of straw hats. I hardly think that anyone's
pastry could be quite so bad as to warrant that description, so I must
be content in this case with three very near misses.)*

    HH   Do you go to school?

    Jane   No.

    HH   Can you write and read?

    Jane   Just a little.

    HH   Who taught you?

    Jane   My mother.

*(We are still fifty-five years before the Act of Parliament which
made schooling compulsory. I take her now to twenty years old, and
again try some questions designed for validation.)*

    HH   Do you know the name of the king?

    Jane   Yes, it is William ... William IV.

*(Close but not quite right. William IV did not take to the throne until
five years later, in 1830. The correct answer would have been George
IV.)*

    HH   Do you have a market where you live?

    Jane   Yes.

    HH   What day of the week do you have the market?

    Jane   Tuesday.

*(The London markets, such as Billingsgate, were operative every
week day. Whether small local markets existed and ran on a weekly
rota basis cannot be discovered from the available records, but it
seems logical that traders would tour the districts of London just as.
they tour provincial towns.)*

    HH   Do you know the name of the Lord Mayor of London?

    Jane   Sir William Foster, I think.

(According to A. B. Beavon's Aldermen of London, *there was no
Lord Mayor of that name at the time in question. But on further
checking, I found there was a 'common councilman' for the Broad
Street Ward by the name of Charles Foster during the exact year of
the interview. At her claimed age of twenty, the year would be 1825:
Foster was councilman for the fifteen years up to 1828.)*

HH   How are you dressed?

Jane   I have got a grey dress of fairly fine wool . . . a long one . . . It is gathered in at the waist and has got a white collar and cuffs.

HH   What kind of shoes are you wearing?

Jane   They are black lace-up to just above the ankles with highish heels. They go in a bit about the middle and come out again.

(Two thousand years may have passed, but her descriptive abilities have not improved much since she tried to direct me from one Greek island to another. What I can make of her description seems fairly accurate, though it is the kind of thing anyone in modern times would not have much difficulty guessing at with equal accuracy. As I take her forward in years, she marries at twenty-four and moves with her husband John Armitage to Margate, Kent. At the age of forty she says they now live in Westgate which is quite close to Margate.

HH   Do you go out a lot? Does John take you to special functions?

Jane   We occasionally go to dinners in the evening and sometimes we go to the theatre . . . it is the Theatre Royal.

Beyond this point, there is little which checks out or can be checked out. At the end, she says she died at the age of sixty-four and was buried at St Catherine's Church, Westgate. This seems rather odd, as she gave her address as St Catherine's Road, not in Westgate but at the time when she was living in Margate. This is the second case of coincidences in the interview, the other being that all three of her homes were in places ending in 'gate'.

I would say that, here again, fantasy figures largely in Rosamund's lives. However, amongst the imaginings lie some interesting facts pointing to a genuine memory. Could the name Ludgate Street have been a wild guess? Could the classical travelogue of the Greek islands have been the invention of an overactive imagination? Could someone playing a Dutch girl as a fictional role suddenly decide to pick a totally different and obscure language for a native tongue – and just happen to pick on the right one? You may feel that the answer is yes, it could be so. You could believe then that the other 'minds' in Rosamund's head are not just part, but all fantasy. You will forgive me, I hope, if I do not join you in that belief.

6

Irene – A Soul Surveys the Aftermath

Many modern hypnotherapists familiar with past life regression believe the state of mind in the present life owes much to the traumatic incidents of lives gone before. In just the same way as a patient's present life will be searched for the roots of existing anxiety, they believe that the search must often go further. Since beginning this project, I myself have turned successfully to past lives in treating my normal day-to-day patients. Take compulsive eating as an example. Where this socially inhibiting problem cannot be blamed on any trauma from the present lifetime, a deeper delve may reveal a surprising explanation.

We forget in our comfortable twentieth century environment how many people even in European countries have known real hunger. It produces in the sufferer a new instinct – an overwhelming drive to eat anything edible within reach without stopping to think about whether there is a need. Why should the victim of starvation need to think, 'do I need to eat' when the answer is always, 'yes'? But, whether that past life be real or fantasy, does its ending also bring an end to the craving? The answer, I have found, is that it definitely does not. Someone whose prime motivation in life was the scratching together of a subsistence is suddenly 'reborn' into a new life. He or she looks around to see a table laid out for dinner . . . and a pantry . . . and a freezer . . . and a cake shop. The age-old urge is rekindled, and the girth suffers the inevitable consequence.

In the case of Irene, the matter is rather different, however. Firstly, of course, she was a volunteer with no problems, not a patient with a need for a cure. Where her story touches on the psychological aspects of regression is in the trends carried on from each of her past lives into the next. Fortunately for her, none of these 'family' traits has carried on into her present life, and there is nothing I can find in her present life which might cause fantasies of this nature to occur. She is the only subject of the core of five who has transcended the gender barrier, that is, the only one to have memories of being both man and woman. In fact, in her five useful past lives, plus one which was too short for our purposes, she has alternated from male to female. That sequence is broken only when she moved from the dead child – a girl – to her present life. This raises the question of the purpose behind this phenomenon. Perhaps there was some mysterious need for this alteration – a need which was not fulfilled by the fatal age of six, so she had to have another go at being a woman.

Another trend occurs with the occupation in the male lives and the painful way in which two of them died. Two of the three men were soldiers and the third had a hankering for the military life but was kept in 'civies' by a slight disablement. Even more odd is the way those two military careers ended – both with a blade in the belly. Some may say this is phallic in origin, others that such a painful, almost ritual death represents the self-scourging fantasy of someone believing they deserve such punishment. Both those diagnoses would only be valid on the assumption that this 'past' is merely a subconscious reflection of the present, expressed symbolically as in a dream. And they would, in that case, have to be backed up by some evidence of cause in the present life, and nothing of the sort was apparent in the case of Irene.

The second psychologically interesting point is her behaviour as a woman when faced with imminent marriage. As a carefree gipsy girl, she suddenly demands to be brought back to the present rather than face the wedding night. The explanation of this is rather less sinister than one would first imagine, as I later discovered in conversation with Irene. We know that a subject in full regression is fully immersed in the particular life and time and the thoughts, visions and feelings that go with it. But on top of this there seems to be a curious cross-pollenation of those thoughts with the knowledge gained in later lives right up to the present. While the subject gives the appearance of being one hundred per cent in the mind of the earlier life, there is still some link with the present which, for example, allows an ancient Greek to converse in English or a mediaeval gipsy to use words like 'Gran'. Irene explained to me later that the same vestige of the present – in this case her happily married self – would not allow her to go through the wedding formalities – or informalities – with another man. It did not seem to make much difference that the man in question died some hundreds of years before her present husband was born.

Because of these characteristics in Irene's interviews, I have concentrated more on this aspect than on the usual validation work. Also, as you will see, the circumstances of some of her lives would make more than a basic validation search impossible anyway.

Irene does have one other quality of note, in that, including the child-death, she has produced both the earliest and the latest life in the project. She begins five centuries before Rosamund's Andromache when she is Sorab, the son of an Egyptian scribe. Sent to help his father, he begins by describing the bustle of the market scene:

Sorab It is very busy ... a lot of noises going on. There is shouting and people selling things ... horses and soldiers and women and children ... standing watching at the moment. I have to – I should be doing something. Better hurry. What did I come for? I was sent to get something. By mother.

HH Who rules over the land of Egypt?

Sorab Ramases.

HH Is he the first King Ramases?

Sorab No, it is the third one we have had.

(*This would date Sorab to about 1,000 BC. After this, he goes without request into a description of the soldiers of Ramases's court.*)

Sorab Golden, like the sun.

HH What is?

Sorab The staffs they carry ... and their head dresses are beautiful.

HH Would you like to be soldier when you grow up?

Sorab I don't know ... It's a bit hard being a soldier. You have to be tough. I don't know whether I am tough enough. And I have got a bad foot. Just a little ... it drags. Mother says it will get better as I get older.

HH Have you any brothers or sisters?

Sorab   I have one sister ... Mereksan.
HH   What does your father do?
Sorab   He is a scribe ... He is showing me.
HH   How are you dressed? What clothes are you wearing?
Sorab   Just white linen. It is not really white, it was white, with a tie and a shortish tunic. It is quite scratchy.

(I can only assume that a tie in this context means a form of sash or belt. Taken now to fifteen years old and he is again in some kind of market.)

Sorab   I am in a big hall ... a lot of men exchanging money and goods. Father is writing some of the exchanges down and I am helping. I am writing some.
HH   Do you have to put dates on your transactions?
Sorab   No, just names. Just names.
HH   Where is your mother?
Sorab   At home (*laughing*). One of the chickens has got loose and it is flapping about.
HH   They are selling chickens, are they?
Sorab   Yes ... Sometimes it is for money, sometimes it is for other goods.
HH   What do they call the coins?
Sorab   Sesterces.

(Sadly, one of the few points capable of validation, this, and it is wrong. Sesterces were Roman coins and did not appear until later. Now he goes to twenty years and has begun to conduct business on his own.)

Sorab   I am travelling ... along the road from one place to the next ... It is dusty ... My father is dead ... I am travelling from home to a small village on the outskirts of Thebes to write down some transactions, and someone is selling a house and they want me to write it ... It is very hot and dusty and I am thirsty ... riding a horse ... It is white ... He has got some piebald on him and he is very gentle and he is hot too. There are a lot of flies.
HH   What do you write on?
Sorab   On papyrus ... with a sharpened – a sharpened reed.

(This is quite right, of course, but it is also common knowledge.)

HH   Do you make the ink yourself?

Sorab   Yes, it is made from crushed (*pause*) with water –
         crushed ...
HH   What do you crush?
Sorab   That is what I'm trying to remember.
HH   How much did you have to pay for your horse?
Sorab   I didn't pay for him; I got him for some work I did for
         someone ... because he is not young. I think he has got
         a few years more left.

*(To twenty-five now, and Sorab is dying. The overtures to his death
begin without my realising it. But as the death is a relatively peaceful
and painless one I allow it to continue. At the actual point of death,
Irene's breathing actually stops but there is no danger, as I can
immediately slide her forward into the 'spirit world'.)*

Sorab   I am lying in bed ... Mother is looking after me ... I
         have got a fever. It is making me very hot and I have got
         sores on my body.
HH   Is there a physician to come and look at you?
Sorab   No. We can't afford one at the moment. I have got to
         get better.
HH   How long have you been ill?
Sorab   I don't know. It seems a long time. Mother says it is a
         few days, but I can't remember.
HH   Do you have any pain?
Sorab   Just feel tired, very tired and sore. Finding it very hard
         to breathe ... hot and cold ... (*shows some difficulty in
         breathing*) I have got to get better (*breathing worsens*)
         ... Mother ... (*long pause*) Go away, go away ...
         (*breathing goes fainter then eventually stops*).
HH   Now, time is passing, it is a little later. What is
         happening to you now?
Sorab   Nothing.
HH   Are you still alive?
Sorab   No.
HH   What did they do with your body?
Sorab   Mother put ointments on it and wrapped it in a sheet.
         And then it was taken out of the city and laid beside
         Father ... in a cave.

Irene's pattern of lives now follows similar lines to those of

Rosamund as she jumps about 2,000 years into her next existence. Now she is a girl again, a Romany wanderer in England at a time which is difficult to determine. She herself has no idea of dates or anything by which we can take reference. All we can deduce is that she died prior to 1169, when the subsequent life began. There is one small thread of continuity from her life as Sorab, despite the time lapse because, as she rightly says, the Romanies originate from Egypt. She gives a rather indignant reply when I first ask her if she calls herself a gipsy. I had forgotten that of course the word 'gipsy' was originally a derogatory slang term for Romanies, derived from the word Egyptians. Soon after this, she goes on to give the reason why they have to keep moving around:

HH   Do you call yourself Gipsies?
Alison   No (*sternly*). Romanies, not gipsies.
HH   Can you tell me what is happening?
Alison   Everyone hurrying ... I don't know why, Gran didn't
         say ... just have to hurry ... I don't like hurrying. I like
         being here. I don't know where we are going ... wish
         we were not moving. Still, that's it. I suppose we will
         find somewhere else. It doesn't do to worry. We will be
         all right so long as we stay together. They don't like
         us much – people. I think that is why we are moving.

(*She goes on to say at the age of fifteen that there are nine caravans in their group, then gives us the only real clue to the date.*)

Alison   Ten hundred and summat. I don't know.
HH   Are you still happy?
Alison   No. I don't know why, I should be happy.
HH   Do you not like your father?
Alison   Well, he's all right.
HH   Does he beat you?
Alison   Sometimes. If I don't sell enough. Just depends how
         the mood takes him. It depends how he feels.

(*I return her to an earlier train of thought, that she is at the moment on her way to fetch water.*)

Alison   It is warm ... the sun is nice ... I think I will run back.
         No. I might spill the water. I have to go careful.
HH   Do you wear shoes?
Alison   No.

HH   What sort of clothes do you wear?

Alison   Kirtle ... You know, a skirt and a top and a bodice and
        streamers.

(*The word 'kirtle' appears to have referred to any kind of dress or
over-petticoat. According to etymological dictionaries, the term is
now archaic and dates back to old English. In Alison's day, it would
probably be spelt 'cyrtel'.*)

HH   Are you sunburnt?

Alison   Yes ... and I have got dark hair.

(*We go now to sixteen years old, and she begins with the
preparations for her marriage which, in the case of this interview,
terminates our meeting.*)

Alison   I am with William ... getting married ... soon ... Every-
        one gathers round and we have a special sort of cere-
        mony only for Romanies, and then we are married.

HH   Who performs the ceremony? Do you have a leader?

Alison   Yes, Josh ... He decides were we go ... He looks after
        us.

HH   And he marries you?

Alison   No – it's just everyone all together. They will all be
        there and we are all in together. All the families. And
        we have to do things and then we are married. All
        different things.

(*I move her on to the day of the wedding to hear more of the
ceremony in store. But ...*)

Alison   Everyone is running about ... Everybody is happy,
        dancing and the music. Everything is going on ... I
        don't want to be there any more ... I want to be back
        ... I just want to be back.

HH   Is something wrong?

Alison   No, I just wanted to be back ... in the present, I mean
        ... back to Irene.

HH   Why are you frightened, can you remember?

Irene   (*Still under the hypnosis but I have now brought her out of
        regression.*) I don't want to go back ... I want to stay
        here ... I am frightened I would not be able to come
        back here.

HH   Was it the idea of getting married that upset you?

Irene   I cannot remember.

HH   You don't want to get married?
Irene   Perhaps.

It was only when Irene was brought fully out of her hypnotic
state that she was able to analyse her feelings and the reasons for
her reluctance to indulge in this bigamy of the mind.

Her next life, however, could produce no such problems as,
once again, she becomes a man. Much of the information given by
William Swainby in his short but eventful life is at best confusing
and at worst contrary to known fact. He appears to fight with a
weapon not yet in common use and it also seems he is fighting in
the wrong country. He makes up for this, however, in his
marvellously colourful descriptions of preparing for war and
going into battle, culminating in the eerie but exciting epilogue.
We hear from the mouth of what claims to be the departed spirit,
floating near his still-warm corpse and keeping watch over the
field of battle after the fury is over.

He begins his fighting man's career at just fifteen, in year 1184,
when he joins the army by lying about his age. William tells us he
lives in Wiltshire and is going to Shrewsbury to join up.
Shrewsbury is of course not in Wiltshire, and for that matter
nowhere near, but Salisbury is one of the biggest cities in the
county of Wiltshire and does sound very similar.

William   Going along the road with another lad from the
          village. Laughing ... I am going to join the Army.
HH   Will they let you join when you are fifteen?
William   They won't know ... I am a big lad and as long as I
          can fight they won't care.
HH   What does your father say about you joining the
          army?
(*He has explained earlier that his father is a professional soldier.*)
William   He says I am a fool. But he is hardly there anyway, so
          no matter.
(*Twenty years old now and I ask him where he is.*)
William   In a field. The tents are pitched and it is all muddy
          and dirty.
HH   What do you fight with, William?
William   A pike.
(*First records of the pike being in common use do not occur until*

67

some time later. There is no record of whether it was used occasionally before then. He does add, however, that he is fighting for King Richard and this is correct for the date.)

    William   We are getting ready to go ... We are going over the water ... It is the King, he want to fight ... the infidel. He thinks we should make Christians of them ... We get paid when they remember ... in shillings.

(At twenty-five he has returned home and explains the fighting was in Turkey. The Holy Wars under Richard did indeed extend into Turkey. William is now taking a break at home where he is looking forward to good and regular food. But he is also looking forward to going back to fight and is waiting for his message to return. Five years later he is in action again. He says he is fighting for Richard in Spain, though as far as I can deduce, Richard's war is in France.)

    William   Near Cadiz somewhere – along the plateau ... oh, there are a lot of horses around and we are on foot, but some are on horses. I think we are going to be mown down.

    HH   What weapons are they using – the soldiers?

    William   Swords – great big swords. We have only got our pikes – the horses' feet right in the middle. If we get out ... we will just have to pray to God.

    HH   What is happening now?

    William   There is no way out ... All the blood is coming out ... out of my belly ... a sword thrust – a big sword. Everything is going white – all going away ... All the noises and horses and everything.

(Again, the subject was not showing sufficient emotion to cause any danger, so I made this the second exception and allowed William to live out his life to the very end.)

(As he spoke, Irene herself grew pale. Her face became pained and her knuckles whitened as she gripped her abdomen. Then, the tension was suddenly gone and Irene relaxed again.)

    HH   What are you feeling?

    William   Peaceful, quiet ... I don't know what it is ... There is no pain ... no pain. It is all gone ... starting to float ... gone.

(Irene sighs and William now begins to describe what he can see of his own body.)

William   Just lying.

HH   Is there blood coming from it?

William   Not now.

HH   And will no one move your body?

William   I dare say.

HH   I want you to tell me what happens to your body. Is the battle finished yet?

William   It seems to be ... I think we won ... They are coming on horses to look to see ... They are making some trenches ... yes, and wrapping us in cloth ... There are a lot dead.

HH   They wrap you in cloth do they, like a shroud?

William   Yes, and making the sign of the cross ... English ... The Spanish have gone ... retreated.

HH   Will they bury the Spanish ones as well?

William   Yes, they will take anything useful from them first – they like to have their trophies ... yes, they will bury them.

HH   And when they have taken anything useful will they bury them?

William   Yes.

HH   Not with the English dead?

William   *(Very positively.)* Oh, no, they will give them *(the English)* a Christian burial.

HH   What has happened to your body, anything yet?

William   It has been put in the trench and covered over.

HH   Are there many bodies in the trench?

William   Yes, a lot.

HH   Will they mark it in anyway?

William   They will put a cross on.

HH   Do you know the exact place in Spain where the grave is?

William   On a plateau. Flattened, dry and dusty.

William may be dead, but Irene's soldiering days are far from over. After taking a few centuries rest and a comfortable but uneventful sojourn in the form of Patricia Mountain, she takes her place with the Lancers in World War I. There is little to say of Patricia, the daughter of a knighted gentleman in seventeenth century Sussex, except that the nuptial dread of Alison was avoided in this case by jumping from the fitting of the wedding dress to a point five years later, after the marriage.

Robert Underwood is the brave young Lancer. He lives in Bath (bringing that town's total in the files up to three) from the year 1886.

HH   Do you know the name of the road, the street or road?
Robert Wilmslow Crescent.

(*Present maps show no trace of any Wilmslow Crescent, but there is a street called Williamstowe.*)

HH   How do you spend your time when you are not at school?
Robert Reading ... Oh, nothing frivolous, Daddy would not let me read anything unsatisfactory.

(*He joins the army as a cadet at the age of nineteen and a half. He talks of the red uniforms with gold buttons, and boasts that he has a moustache. The regiment, he says, is the 16th Lancers. When he is twenty I ask him if Victoria is still on the throne as he said she was earlier.*)

Robert No ... Edward.

(*If he is twenty, the year is 1906. Victoria died in 1901 and Edward VII reigned from then until 1910. Robert's rank advances from lance corporal to lieutenant. Then, when he is twenty-eight, comes the Great War and Robert is sent to France. He does not live to see the war enter its second year.*)

HH   Where are you now?
Robert Floating, floating.
HH   Are you alive?
Robert Floating, floating.
HH   Are you dead?
Robert Yes ... a sabre thrust ... in France ... 1914.
HH   Were you killed by a German?
Robert Yes.
HH   Were you on horseback?
Robert No.
HH   On foot?

Robert	Yes ... We were all going forward ... Suddenly there they were ... They came upon us. We didn't know ... The lot were killed.
HH	Where were you pierced by the sabre?
Robert	Under my ribs.
HH	What happened to your body?
Robert	Buried ... near Lyons.
HH	A military cemetery?
Robert	Yes ... I can see the headstone ... white 'Robert Underwood' and then there is something in smaller writing – I am trying to see – 'Died November fourteenth, 1914.'

The 3,000 year thread has one more slight reappearance before it is Irene's turn to see the world, but there was not even enough of it to learn anything by regression. I discovered when cataloguing all the lives that after Robert Underwood came one Jane Atkinson. Because I learned using Guided Visual Imagery that Jane lived to be only six, I took what information I could at that stage. She said that she was born in 1932 but in 1938 contracted diphtheria and died. It is interesting that such a short life is followed by an even shorter gap before she comes into her next, and present, life as Irene. There is, as I have said, not always a correlation between the length of an inter-life period and any of the other time factors surrounding it. But this case, and some others drawn from similar circumstances, do seem to show some consistency where there is evidence of there having been a short physical life. This clearly indicates that whether this is reincarnation or fantasy or whatever your favourite theory, the 'limbo period' serves some function not unlike sleep. Statistical calculations agree with the statement from the 'virgin soul' of my volunteers that the average period between apparent lives is just over fifty years. Perhaps then, an earthly existence, real or otherwise, of a normal lifespan is so tiring to the ever-active mind as to make such hibernation necessary. It would seem logical then that the short and stress-free, simple life of a child should drain the soul far less, and that the brief span of little Jane Atkinson called for only two years of rest before the birth of the woman who is alive today.

7

Sheila – The Case For – and Against

An ancient herbalist, a minstrel, a milliner's daughter and a member of a family of parliamentarians – that was Sheila. But to the project she was something else besides all these. She was the source of the deepest puzzles and the most teasing enigmas of the entire three year study. For while, in at least one life, she overwhelmed with the ampleness and uncanny accuracy of her information, she also provided a steady stream of absolute negatives. Whether you believe that the past life regression phenomenon proves the occurrence of reincarnation or not, Sheila has something to cause you doubt.

The seam of gold she had to offer, as I mentioned in Chapter One, was her most recent past life as Jane Martin. Jane tells us she is the daughter of an M.P. At ten years old, she says she believes his constituency is around the area where she lives – Gloucester. At that age, she does not know his Christian name. After this first interview, I found a James Martin who represented nearby Tewkesbury around that time, but at a second interview, after the validation documents had all been collected, she decided his name was John. This may at first seem disappointing, but further examination of the Martin family showed that four successive generations had brothers James and John, most of whom had held the Tewkesbury seat at some time in their lives. But then she began to mention other names, most of which seem to show the same uncanny closeness to the target, but never a direct hit. As well as both names for her father, Jane maps out a family tree which includes two Roberts and a Penelope. If we turn to the documented history of the Martin family around that century, we find three Penelopes and a Robert as well as the four Jameses and Johns. In fact, if we are to accept the dates given, with the first interview stated to be in 1801 – then the Martin in Parliament at that time, James, did indeed marry a Penelope. And Jane, who claims to be his daughter, says her mother is called Margaret Penelope. See how the actual Martin family tree compares with Jane's version from her second interview:

THE MARTINS ACCORDING TO RECORDS MADE AT THE TIME

James   John
             (1692–1767,
             M.P. 1741–47)

John   Joseph   James = Penelope
(1724–94,   (M.P. 1774–96)   (1738–1810,
M.P. 1754–61)   M.P. 1776–1807)

                  'several sisters'
                  (at least four)

James   Penelope   Eliza   Anne   Joseph   John = Frances
                                             (1774–1832,
                                             M.P. 1812–32)

       Robert   Penelope   James   John   Emily   Frances

THE MARTINS ACCORDING TO JANE

Henry = Charlotte   John/James = Margaret Penelope
                         (c 1764 – ?)

         Robert   Jane = James Booth

           Robert   Charlotte   Margaret

The name of Penelope, Jane's mother, according to her second interview, provided an interesting and refreshing twist in what is often a long and dry process – instant validation. The team had researched the Martin family thoroughly after the first interview, and by the time Sheila took to the couch a second time I already knew the correct answer to a question I could put to her. There was no possibility of Sheila having heard the information during the research process. Each life was checked by a different researcher, and great care was taken to avoid accidental collusion between the researcher and the hypnosis volunteer. So, unknown to Sheila, when she told me in her second interview she was the daughter of the Tewkesbury M.P. whose wife was called Penelope, I already had that information in my files.

Jane sets the scene in her first interview at the age of ten, telling us she is sitting on her rocking horse in the nursery of her home in Berkley, near Gloucester. It is May and she is happy. The year is 1801 and she tells us the country is under the reign of King George (*correct*).

HH   Where is your father?
Jane   He is away ... gone to London.
HH   What does he do in London?
Jane   Parliament.

(*She goes on at this age and at fifteen to say she thinks he is Gloucester's M.P., the name of the house is Hinderwell, and she has a brother Robert who is two years older than herself. Now she is twenty years old.*)

HH   Is anything happening?
Jane   I am going to London.
HH   With your parents?
Jane   Mm ... for a holiday ... next week.
HH   Is Robert going too?
Jane   No ... he is at school.

(*Twenty-five years old now and Jane says she is on a farm in Crediton, Devon, where she now lives.*)

HH   Have you left Berkley? Have you married?
Jane   Yes ... James Booth ... He has a farm ... I was twenty-five.
HH   Do you have any children yet?
Jane   Yes ... two ... a girl ... two years old ... Charlotte ... James is three.
HH   Are you happy on the farm? Is it a big farm?
Jane   Yes ... quite big ... Rowden Farm.
HH   Rowden Farm? How do you spell it?
Jane   R-O-W-D-E-N.

(*Research has shown there was, and indeed still is, a Rowden Farm in the parish of Witheridge, quite close to Crediton. Dating back in records to 1285, Rowden Farm is now listed by the Department of the Environment as a building of historical or architectural interest.*

The present buildings are said to be seventeenth century. Jane is now thirty.)

    HH   Where are you now?

    Jane   In the drawing room ... doing my embroidery.

    HH   Have you had any more children?

    Jane   A little girl ... Margaret ... She is two.

    HH   Are you still on the farm?

    Jane   No ... fire.

    HH   Did it burn down?

    Jane   Yes.

    HH   Anybody hurt?

    Jane   Yes ... James.

    HH   Is that your son or your husband?

    Jane   Both.

    HH   Were they killed?

    Jane   Yes.

    HH   How many years ago?

    Jane   Three.

    HH   So you would be twenty-seven when it happened?

    Jane   No. Thirty.

    HH   You are thirty now – or are you?

    Jane   Thirty-five.

    HH   It was three years ago, so you were thirty-two?

    Jane   Yes.

    HH   Where are they buried? Were they buried?

    Jane   No.

    HH   Could they not find the bodies?

    Jane   No.

    HH   Where are you living now?

    Jane   Exeter ... with an uncle ... Robert ... Robert Booth.

    HH   Do you know the address?

    Jane   Cranleigh House ... fairly large ... just outside Exeter.

(Jane passes to forty years old when she tells us she has a bad cough. I pass her to a later time in the same year.)

    HH   Tell me what is happening to you now? (*a long pause.*)
             Are you still there? ... have you died?

    Jane   Yes.

    HH   What was the cause of your death, Jane?

    Jane   A plaguy cough.

HH   Where did they bury your body?
Jane   St Mary's ... Exeter.
(*Exeter has three churches of that name dating back to Jane's time –
St Mary Major, St Mary Arches and St Mary Steps. But searches
into all three sets of parish records have found no burial of anyone by
that name.*)

After the matter-of-fact interview to establish the traceable
basics of Jane's life, let us now look at the second discussion with
Jane. Nearly two years of present-day time separate the two
interviews, and remember that Sheila has seen or heard nothing of
the feedback from her first up to the time of the second. This time,
Jane begins at twenty years old. After she describes Hinderwell
House as standing alone with a nice garden, she says her father's
Christian name is John, and at first simply says her mother is
called Margaret.

HH   Margaret? Is that her only Christian name?
Jane   I don't think so.
HH   Does she have another one? Do you know what it is?
Jane   It's Penelope.
HH   Do you have any brothers or sisters?
Jane   I have a brother Robert ... I think he's gone abroad ...
        I think he's in France ... He's about twenty-two.
(*She tells us again that there is a George on the throne. This time she
identifies him as George III and goes on to repeat that her father is
an MP.*)
HH   For what area?
Jane   I think it's for Tewkesbury. But it's the surrounding
        area as well.
HH   Do you have any uncles or aunts who visit you?
Jane   I have an Uncle Henry ... Aunt Charlotte ... They have
        one son ... cousin.
(*Henry is her father's brother, she tells us, and she believes all her
grandparents are dead.*)
HH   Are you a pretty girl Jane? What colour are your eyes?
Jane   Yes, I think so, quite pretty. Blue.
HH   Have you ever been away from Berkley?
Jane   We went to London ... We went to some balls. And
        looked at shops and went to some parks ... I saw some

famous people. I didn't exactly meet them ... the Prince
Regent, I saw ... George.

HH He's not the King?

Jane No. (*inaudible*) King George. I didn't see him.

HH But you saw the Prince Regent? Is he a very attractive
man?

Jane He's getting a bit fat ... He dresses quite nicely. Bright
colours ... There were lots of people that I met.

HH Did you meet any other Members of Parliament?

Jane I met Mr Percival.

HH He's a friend of your father's, is he?

Jane I don't know about a friend. I think they know one
another, but I don't think they're that friendly.

HH Perhaps they're on opposite sides of the house?

Jane I don't think so.

HH What do they call the parties, the main political parties?

Jane Tories and Whigs.

HH Do you do anything much? Do you go out much?

Jane Sometimes I go out. Sometimes people come to call ...
We've been to parties locally and people come to the
house.

(*She says they have five or six servants. There was also a governess
for Jane's education, but she no longer comes.*)

HH Do you have a young man?

Jane (*sigh*) ... James Booth ... He lives at Crediton in
Devonshire ... He stays in Berkley sometimes ... He
has friends in Berkley ... He's twenty-three ... He came
to Hinderwell House ... He's a farmer ... He owns the
farm ... It was his father's.

HH Are you engaged to be married? Or anything formal?

Jane No.

HH How many times have you met?

Jane Only twice at Hinderwell House, but often in the
grounds of the house.

HH Do you think he will ask you to marry him ... or has he
already asked you?

Jane Yes.

HH Did you accept him?

Jane Yes.

HH   When shall you marry?

Jane   We have to get away from here first ... My parents don't approve.

HH   Will you elope?

Jane   Yes, I think so ... I haven't thought about it yet.

HH   Does his farm have a name?

Jane   Yes (*inaudible*).

HH   Have you been there?

Jane   No.

HH   Your father doesn't want you to marry him?

Jane   No ... He thinks I should do better.

HH   Does your brother know? What's he doing in France?

Jane   I don't know, he's wandering about, I think.

HH   Does he get an allowance?

Jane   He used to. I don't think he does now.

HH   What sort of dialect do the people in your part of the world use? Can you say some of the dialect?

Jane   I don't think so. I'm not very good at imitating voices. I think it's what you call a soft sort of dialect, not like the Welsh.

HH   Is Berkley big enough to have a market, a weekly market?

Jane   Oh yes, I think it has a small weekly market, but I don't go to it.

HH   What day of the week do they hold the market, do you know?

Jane   I think it's on the Wednesday.

(*I take Jane to twenty-five, when she is living on Rowden Farm with James, now her husband. She takes up the dramatic story of the lover's elopement.*)

Jane   I escaped from the house one night ... when there was a party. I said I had a headache. Then I went out the back stairs, the servant's way.

(*See what happens now when I give her lover the wrong name: she picks up my mistake immediately.*)

HH   And was John waiting for you?

Jane   (*Very puzzled.*) Pardon?

HH   James, I'm sorry. Was James waiting for you?

Jane   Mm ... with a carriage.

HH   How many horses did the carriage have?
Jane   Two ... side by side ... and a roof.
HH   What do they call that type of carriage?
Jane   I think it was a –

(*The next word sounded at first like 'brown', until I learned later that there was a type of carriage named after its designer, Brougham, pronounced 'browm'.*)

HH   And how long were you before you were married? Were
       you married from Rowden?
Jane   Mm.
HH   Which church did you attend for your wedding?
Jane   We didn't ... I was married at the farm ... It was a priest
       that James got ... He stayed at the farm for a few days
       ... It was Father Thomas ... I think he travelled about
       Devon and Cornwall.
HH   Do a lot of people get married in their home?
Jane   Some do, but most of them don't.

(*She now tells us that she is twenty-six, not twenty-five as directed, and was married at twenty-one. She introduces us again to her children, Charlotte, Margaret and Robert and says she spends her days doing housework and looking after the children.*)

HH   Is it a big farm?
Jane   It's quite big ... It's been in the family for quite a while,
       I think.
HH   You don't know in which century it was built?
Jane   I think it was 1630 or something like that.

(*Once again, this information was confirmed to me prior to this interview, unknown to Sheila. As I said earlier, the present building is D.o.E. listed as seventeenth century.*)

HH   How did your parents take the news?
Jane   Not very pleased. I haven't seen them since.
HH   What about your brother?
Jane   I think he was killed in France.
HH   Has there been a war?
Jane   No, I think he was duelling, I think so.
HH   Time is passing again. Five years have passed ... How
       old are you now, Jane? (*Very long pause; she becomes a
       little restless.*)

HH   What's the matter, Jane? Are you unhappy?

Jane   Yes ... James is gone ... and so is Robert ... They're dead in the fire ... It burnt the farm ... a few years ago.

HH   What happened? Were they not able to save the farm?

Jane   No. Had a thatched roof, you see, went very quickly.

HH   Was your husband not able to get out of the house?

Jane   He was out of the house at the time. He was in the barn ... I was in the house.

HH   So have you rebuilt the farmhouse, then, or what?

Jane   No.

HH   So where do you live?

Jane   With an uncle of James's ... near Exeter ... a house on its own.

HH   What do they call the house, do you know?

Jane   Egglemont, I think. We've been in one or two houses, we haven't always been in this one.

HH   Is James's uncle married?

Jane   No ... bachelor ... Robert ... Robert Booth.

(*Jane now says she doesn't go outside much because she is in poor health.*)

Jane   I've got a bad chest. It's the smoke, I think, from the fire.

HH   Is it a smokey fire?

Jane   No. The one that burnt down the farm. I haven't been very well since then.

HH   Do you ever hear from your parents?

Jane   No. I don't think they're alive now.

HH   Time is passing ... It is now forty years since you were born ... Tell me where you are. (*pause*) Are you still alive?

Jane   No.

HH   What happened to Jane Booth?

Jane   She was buried ... St Mary's ... in Exeter.

HH   Was it just called St Mary's?

Jane   As far as I know. I never went there.

Having discussed what of Jane's family tree resembles that of the Martin family from records, there remains the most significant point, as yet unmentioned. That is the apparent absence of Jane. Her semi-accurate family roll-call ties in very nicely with history but seems at first glance to be quite inaccurate with regard to herself. The first observation from the archival family tree is that nowhere in any of its branches is there a Jane to be found. Simply to say that Jane did not exist would be the first and most obvious conclusion. But at the risk of seeming overzealous and trying to rescue an otherwise dead end, let me submit a couple of other possibilities. The second generation of Martins, (John II, Joseph and James II, sons of John I) also had 'several sisters', probably four or more, according to Bennet's *History of Tewkesbury*. Yet, probably due to the social status afforded to women at the time, no attempt is made to name them. Is it possible that we are one generation out, and poor Jane has made no greater mark on history than as a quarter part of a vaguely titled 'several'? Or perhaps the historians have taken even less trouble elsewhere and simply left her out. Or there is one third possibility, which has a certain romantic appeal as well as a very ready credibility. Jane tells us how she was virtually cut off from her family when she married below her station, through love of the young farmer James Booth. It needs little imagination to read the feelings of her Hon. father towards his daughter's relatively rustic suitor. For him to ostricise his daughter as a result of the liaison he must have felt a deep and strong resentment against the young man and his social standing. Could it be that the M.P.'s shame led him even to strike a child of his own from the family records? All these theories are mere guesses to raise a spark of hope for the validity of Jane, but I do feel they should be considered as candidates for wedging ajar the door of possibility.

But enough of Jane for the moment. We now follow Sheila back through time to the next of her four lives. Next we eavesdrop on a young French girl named Jeanette Cartier and her short life as she follows her parents' search for a new homeland. She opens her interview on board ship at the age of ten as she crosses the English Channel with her family, who are embarking on their first emigration.

Jeanette	Leaning on the rail … it is a sailing ship.
HH	Where is it sailing to?
Jeanette	Southampton, England.
HH	Do you know what year it is?
Jeanette	1719.
HH	Is your home in France?

Jeanette   Not now.
HH   Whereabouts in France did you live?
Jeanette   Paris ... I am going to England ... going to join an
           uncle and aunt.
HH   Are they English or French?
Jeanette   French.
HH   Where do your aunt and uncle live in England?
Jeanette   Bath.

*(She now tells us she is travelling with her father, mother and brother
for her father to carry on his trade as a hatter in the city. He was a
hatter in Paris but Jeanette does not know the reason for the
upheaval. They are sailing on a ship called the Mont Blanc,
captained by a Frenchman named Marchant. I take her to eleven
years old now and ask her where she is.)*

Jeanette   In a drawing room ... over a shop ... on Pulteney
           Bridge ... number ten, Pulteney Bridge.

*(There is a Pulteney Bridge in the city of Bath. But the existing
bridge was not built until 1770, and there is no record of any bridge
on the site previous to that, although it was ferried.)*

Jeanette   It is a millinery shop.
HH   What is your uncle's name?
Jeanette   Cartier ... Pierre Cartier.
HH   What is your aunt's name?
Jeanette   Matilde.
HH   And your mother and father?
Jeanette   Jean Paul ... Martha.
HH   Your father, where does he make the hats?
Jeanette   At the back of the milliner's shops.
HH   Ladies' hats or men's?
Jeanette   He makes men's hats.
HH   And how do you spend your time now that you are
           eleven?
Jeanette   I help in the shop sometimes ... and I have lessons in
           the back of the shop.
HH   Do you know the name of the King of England?
Jeanette   George (*correct*).
HH   Do you speak in English or French?
Jeanette   Sometimes French, sometimes English ... English is
           easier now ... I learnt some before I left France.

HH   Do you know any French poems?

(at the mention of poetry, Jeanette recites a short verse by La Fontaine based on one of Aesop's fables. But, mysteriously, I did not at first know its source and was not even able to have it translated. When I played the tape to English graduates in the French language they could not even understand her mode of speech. But then came the surprise. I had made the mistake of expecting students of adult text book French to be conversant with a child's street language. It was only by chance that I played the same section of tape to an eleven year old French child who was visiting us at the time. She grasped the whole poem on first hearing and was able to interpret it immediately into written French. This is what she gave me:)

> *Monsieur le Corbeau sur un arbre perché,*
> *Tenait dans son bec un fromage,*
> *Monsieur le Renard par l'odeur alléché.*
> *Et bonjour, M. le Corbeau que vous êtes joli que*
> *vous me semblez beau.*
> *M. le Corbeau sur un arbre perché,*
> *Tenait dans son bec un fromage.*
> I can't remember any more.

(At twelve years old, Jeanette says the shop is prospering. When she is thirteen she is making boxes for her father's hats. Little changes until four years later when we rejoin her in a coach with her father and mother.)

HH   Where are you going?

Jeanette   To Plymouth ... We are going on a ship ... America.

HH   Why do you want to go to America?

Jeanette   It's a new country.

(A little later the same year now, and she is aboard the Marie Therese sailing across the Atlantic.)

Jeanette   I am not well ... I have got a fever.

HH   What does your mother think is the matter?

Jeanette   She doesn't say.

HH   Are you getting any medicine for it?

Jeanette   No.

HH   Now it is a little later still. Where are you? (*pause*) ...
          Jeanette, where are you? (*long pause*) Are you dead?

Jeanette   Yes ... a week.

HH   What have they done with your body?
Jeanette In the water.
HH   Who dropped your body in the water?
Jeanette Sailors.
HH   Did many people die?
Jeanette Yes.
HH   What do you feel? Can you see anything?
Jeanette Cold and green.

Now we move back to our next life in Sheila's historical chain. As Elizabeth De Bois, the mediaeval travelling player, she again gives us a wealth of checkable and indeed accurate information. But because of the greater elapse of time and Elizabeth's nomadic lifestyle, her own life has few of those 'hooks' in history which could prove whether she herself or her family ever existed. Her house was a tent, her home was simply wherever she happened to be. But, as if to offset that, the initial and later in-depth interviews with this free spirit are full of a warmth and character that put much living flesh on the bones of our established mental pictures. She describes for example what little value was put on life in the thirteenth century, especially the life of a mere minstrel. In the second interview we hear how her first and only lover was killed defending her honour against lecherous drunken soldiers, leaving her with nothing but the most casual apology from the nobleman in charge.

Elizabeth is a girl of partly French lineage, hence the surname, which would be fairly common in post-Norman England. This trend of course continues through the nobility she mentions, and it is widely known that the Conqueror's kinsmen took over the aristocracy and held a virtual monopoly of it for many generations after the invasion of 1066.

In the outline interview, Elizabeth begins in 1223 at the age of ten by telling us she travels the country in a group of about twenty assorted entertainers. She herself acts, dances and plays the harp, and tells us later that her singing voice is not really up to performing standard. She is one of six or seven children in the band. We join her now, five years later, and at the moment the band is camped at Winchester:

HH   How long will you be staying at Winchester?

Elizabeth Maybe a week or two.
HH   Where will you go after Winchester? (*no response*)
          Where do you get your food from, the market or the
          taverns?
Elizabeth From the markets when we are in the towns.
HH   What do you buy at the market, mostly vegetables,
          or meat?
Elizabeth Both.
HH   What would be the price of a hen or chicken?
Elizabeth Sometimes we barter things.
HH   What would you barter for a chicken?
Elizabeth Maybe we would dance.
HH   What time of year is it?
Elizabeth June.
HH   Are you happy or sad?
Elizabeth Happy.
HH   Where do you sleep?
Elizabeth We have tents.
HH   Do you perform in plays?
Elizabeth Sometimes ... comedies ... The players write them
          sometimes.
HH   Time is passing ... Five years have gone by ... Now
          you are twenty. Where are you, Elizabeth?
Elizabeth Lincoln ... very big.
HH   Do you know the name of the King?
Elizabeth Henry ... Henry III.
(*Correct. He reigned 1216–1272.*)
HH   Do they have things like a theatre, or do you just
          perform in the square or something?
Elizabeth Sometimes we perform in the cathedral ... some-
          times inside ... sometimes out.
HH   Will the Bishop allow you to perform your plays in
          the cathedral?
Elizabeth Yes, if they are religious.
HH   I see. How do you learn these plays?
Elizabeth Parts are written down. Sometimes we just remem-
          ber them.

(*I take her to thirty years old now and she is in Chichester. Her
parents have died of a fever – she thinks it was smallpox. The same*

fever took many other members of their troupe, and other entertainers joined to take their place.)

HH	Where did they come from, from the town?
Elizabeth	Another band of players joined ours.
HH	What do you call yourselves? Do you have a name for the band?
Elizabeth	The Wessex Players.
HH	The Wessex Players. There will be about twenty of you now?
Elizabeth	About twenty-four, I think.
HH	Still sleeping in tents?
Elizabeth	Yes.

(*Now I take her to forty years old, but the only response I can get is a deep sigh. So we carry on to fifty, when she says she is too old for the band and has settled in the village of Bosham, which is near Chichester. She is now employed as a cook.*)

HH	In a big house?
Elizabeth	Not very big ... Ford House.
HH	Does it stand alone?
Elizabeth	No ... by a ford.
HH	Do you like working as a cook?
Elizabeth	I don't mind.
HH	Now five years have passed since I spoke to you last. Tell me what is happening? (*no reply*) Are you alive? (*no reply*) Now you are going back in time ... you are fifty-three, Elizabeth ... Are you still alive?
Elizabeth	Yes.
HH	Are you ill?
Elizabeth	No.
HH	Now time is passing again ... You are fifty-four years old ... Are you still alive?
Elizabeth	Dead ... strange fever.
HH	And where did they bury your body?
Elizabeth	In a churchyard ... in Bosham. Just the church in Bosham.

After such a promising opener, a follow-up was essential. This time, after starting Elizabeth at fifteen years old and re-establishing the basics, such as the correct prefix of her surname (notice the more unusual De Bois instead of Du Bois), I condition her to free-float forwards in time and stop at any exciting or memorable point. She begins when she is standing on a tower at Portchester, looking out at a group of islands. She explains that the Players are going to spend the winter in the grounds of Portchester Castle.

HH   You don't travel in winter?

Elizabeth   Not usually.

HH   Who owns the castle?

Elizabeth   The baron. I don't know his name. I think it's Guy.

HH   Where will you be?

Elizabeth   In a corner of the hall ... Some will be in tents ... I think I have to go and sleep in the tents ... It is too smokey in the castle ... It makes me cough ... The fire in the big fireplace ... logs ... It is very windy and it blows the smoke back in. I cannot see across the hall sometimes. I will have to go to one of the halls near ... It is where the air comes in and the smoke does not come out much.

HH   What are you feeling at the moment?

Elizabeth   A bit colder. I am going down the staircase. I am going out to the tents. There are a lot of stairs and it is cold after you leave the hall. It is snowing a bit ... It is very cold (*coughing*).

HH   What is happening now ... how old are you?

Elizabeth   It is spring ... Sixteen ... Winchester ... We are at the cathedral ... There is a fair on ... with lots of people ... We are going to do some singing and dancing ... in front of the cathedral ... It is a bit of a courtyard, but there is some grass round it too ... Sometimes they give us coins, but sometimes they just invite us for food and things and shelter.

HH   Can you tell me about the cathedral? What sort of place is it? Have you been inside?

Elizabeth   Yes. It is very large ... quite dark inside ... quite cold and it has got some nice windows in it, but it is not very ornate. It's a bit plain ...

(*She floats forward again until romance appears in the life of*

Elizabeth. But as we see, it is short-lived and ends tragically.)

Elizabeth Robert joined us at Winchester.

HH Is he a player?

Elizabeth He is now.

HH Where are you now?

Elizabeth At Lincoln ... We are going to perform at the castle ... at a banquet ... I shall play the harp ... I don't sing much. They will do a mime and a play.

HH Who has ordered this banquet?

Elizabeth It is the local baron, I think ... They have someone staying there – a guest. I think it is Sir William De Palance. There is a table at the far end. It has gold and silver dishes ... and a linen cloth. The other tables haven't. They are just bare and have wooden dishes.

(She floats again, this time into a drama. She has probably only hopped a short time, as they are still in Lincoln and De Palance is still around.)

Elizabeth No. I will not go out. Not going ... I am going to stay here.

HH Who wants you to go outside?

Elizabeth The man with the sword ... I am not going ... I won't go. I am getting annoyed now but I still won't go. He is drunk, I think. They are fighting now. They will not get back into the corner ... They think they are taking me outside – they are not!

HH Why?

Elizabeth Why do you think? ... Now he has got one of the knives from the table ... He has thrown it and it has gone ... I don't want to look anymore ... He is dead now ... Robert ... a sword ... Soldiers from the other end of the room have come and taken the men away ... taken from the hall and I have to go up to the top table. De Palance says he is sorry for the trouble ... The men will not come back ... They have taken them to the dungeons. He says he is sorry it happened ... That's too late now ... Cannot do anything about it now ... It is too late ... The players are taking him away ... I am going to bury

him somewhere in the castle grounds. I don't want
to think about it any more. He is gone. It is finished.

HH   Was he your first lover or did you have one before.

Elizabeth   Robert was the first ... Now he's dead.

(She becomes restless at the tragedy she has to recount, so I take her forward again. She settles sixteen years later, and although the misery of Robert's death is long behind, she is reminded of it by a second meeting with Sir William De Palance.)

Elizabeth   I think we are nearly at our destination. We are
            going to Goodrich ... It is in the West Country
            somewhere ... Not far from Worcester ... You go
            near Worcester to get there ... Goodrich Castle ... I
            think the Welsh had it ... The King is there now ...
            Henry III ... There is going to be a big celebration
            ... We are going to perform ... and the King is there
            ... I think they have taken the castle from the
            Welsh, and I think the King is going to give it to
            William De Palance ... I think he fought along the
            Welsh border and that is why ... because the castle
            is across the border and the Welsh come across
            sometimes.

(Goodrich, on the English/Welsh border near Monmouth, did indeed feature, as Elizabeth says, in the wars of the time.)

HH   You have mentioned William De Palance before,
            haven't you?

Elizabeth   Yes ... Lincoln ... where Robert was killed ... It
            seems just like yesterday.

(I slide her forward just a little, to the actual celebration, and ask her about the King.)

Elizabeth   He's thinnish. Yes, he has a beard ... medium height.

HH   Dark hair?

Elizabeth   Sort of brownish.

HH   Does he wear a crown or anything?

Elizabeth   Mmm ... a small gold one with some red and green
            stones in it.

(The description, both of the man and the crown, seem to tally closely with modern impressions based on what documentation has survived.)

He is – I don't know how to describe it – he really
doesn't seem to take a lot of part in the celebration.
A bit thoughtful, I suppose.

HH   How old do you think he is?

Elizabeth About thirty something I should think.

*(He was born in 1207, she in 1211, therefore as she is now thirty-four
Henry will be thirty-nine or forty years old.)*

HH   Do you recognise anyone else at the top table?

Elizabeth William De Palance ... He is dark ... beard ... He is
taller than the King. The Queen is there ... Eleanor
... She is younger than the King ... about twenty,
twenty-two ... blondish ... quite fair ... a sort of
golden colour.

HH   Is her hair long or short?

Elizabeth It is long ... with no stones in her crown ... gold.

HH   Have you performed?

Elizabeth I played the harp.

HH   Is it a big harp?

Elizabeth Yes. It takes three of the players to carry it into the
hall ... The tunes I make up myself.

HH   Did the King say anything afterwards?

Elizabeth They don't usually say anything. Not to us. We just
provide the entertainment while they eat and afterwards. But if they don't like it you get to know ... It
depends on the tempers ... (*laughing*) ... They
might fling you down the stairs if they do not like it.
If it is really bad. If it is good they give us good food
after the banquet.

*(Moving on again now, this time two years and she is at a tournament
near Winchester, but this time she is only a spectator.)*

HH   What is happening at this tournament, then?

Elizabeth It is jousting ... the King is there ... Henry.

HH   Does the King have any sons?

Elizabeth Yes, I think he has several. And I think he has one or
two daughters as well. There are several there but I
don't know exactly who they are. I think they are his
sons ... And there is somebody they call Simon De
Montfort.

(Forward in time again. Now she thinks she is about fifty-two

and has left the band working in Bosham.)

Elizabeth   Some news came today ... We don't get much news in Bosham, but some came today. The barons have been fighting again and Simon De Montfort has formed a band on London. They are going to govern the country.

HH   Instead of the King?

Elizabeth   The King? It is the barons that rule more than the King.

(If she is about fifty-two, then the year is somewhere around 1263. She has just given an impeccable description of the De Montfort Rebellion, which took place from 1261 to 1265. The rebellion by the Barons under De Montfort's leadership led to the Baron's War from 1263 to 1265. The fighting ended with De Montfort governing the country, but his triumph was short lived. When he died later that year the other barons, robbed of their figurehead, subsided and Henry regained his Throne.)

HH   Has it been a happy life on the whole?

Elizabeth   No, I don't think so.

HH   What would you change?

Elizabeth   Bring back Robert.

HH   Have there been any other lovers since?

Elizabeth   No.

HH   Right through your life, he was your only lover?

Elizabeth   I don't know. I might have when I was drunk but I don't remember any.

HH   Do you get drunk very often?

Elizabeth   Yes, quite often. I drink wine when I can get it.

And so ends the second earliest of Sheila's four past lives. Her earliest life, that of Morag the healer, is from our point of view similar in many ways. She predates any records of ordinary individuals and led a similar nomadic lifestyle. But, like Elizabeth, she makes up for this in other ways. In Morag's case the compensation is in the fine detail with which she illustrates the social and political history of her time. To make the most of this, I summoned Morag for interview three times over a period of thirteen months. And now, to help see her more clearly in her own right rather than simply as another past facet of Sheila, I have decided to dedicate a complete chapter to what she has to tell us.

8
Morag – The Mystic

As we follow each string of lives further back into the past, the job of finding any proof of existence on a personal level becomes increasingly difficult. Even in such relatively recent times as when Jane Martin lived – or claims to have lived – there would have been little hope of tracing her family without her father's prominence to leave clues in history. So what evidence could a life as obscure and far away as Morag's possibly have to offer? No one will probably ever know whether there was such a woman by that name or any other.

Conversely, the history books bulge with the kind of information at the other end of the scale – the most impersonal kind that is common knowledge in every grammar school history class – but that is obviously useless to us. How can we trace a fact in someone's mind to the point where it entered that mind, when the fact is shared by half the adult world?

But somewhere along the line between these two is where Morag's value lies. Throughout the length of three extensive interviews, this wise and mystical figure is a never-ending source of chronicles of her times. And with the possible exception of exact dates that information has proven to be uncannily accurate in virtually every aspect. This modern day woman, who freely admits to having the very minimum of historical learning, has given us more facts in greater depth than we could expect from many who have made a specialist study of the period. The family tree of Alfred the Great is given instantly and accurately, right down to such details as his father's so-called second wife and the order in which his father and brothers acceded to the throne.

Morag herself is a mystery to us as the mystic she claims to be fits none of our stereotypes. The only description she can give of her status is of one who 'has learnt the mysteries'. This woman, who lived as an outcast even within a group of outcasts, tells us of her strange power over animals yet denies being a witch. Whatever she admits or denies, it is clear that the people around her were in no doubt that she was in some way not like them. She describes how she lives amidst a kind of vagrant tribe, and the main pleasure life can hold is a full belly. She is an orphan who has been adopted by a woman named Verna, apparently a wise woman to whom Morag is a kind of apprentice. The time is the ninth century. The name 'Morag', incidentally, is thought to have been in use at that time. Originating from Gaelic/French, it means 'great'.

At twenty she gives us the reason why the travellers must keep on the move. The Saxons, it seems, forbid them settling anywhere, though she does not know why. Not only rejected along with the other travellers, she is also bound to chastity by a further rejection within the group, 'I shall not marry. I am not one of them: there would be trouble'.

Let Morag herself take up the story at the stage in the outline interview where she is thirty years old. She says the travellers are camped near a city:

HH   Do you know the name of the city?
Morag   Bristowe.
HH   Bristowe or Bristol?
Morag   It is Roman. Bristowe.
(*This is one of the archaic names for Bristol dating to this period. Remains found in the modern city show that it does indeed have Roman roots.*)
HH   What are the travelling people doing there?
Morag   Camped on the outskirts and trading with the people in the city.
HH   You are growing older ... Now you are forty years old ... Are you still with the travelling people?
Morag   No ... in a cave.
HH   Alone?
Morag   Except for the hounds.
HH   Why did you leave the tribe?
Morag   My time had come ... They had taught me the mysteries.

HH   Now you live alone in a cave ... Where is the cave?

Morag In the hills ... south west ... Nearby there is a settle-
         ment ... Cadman.

(*It is difficult to tell whether she said Cadman or Cadnam. But in the
later interviews she says Cadnam and this is the traceable one. The
best known place of that name is a small town in the New Forest, but
that is the south of England, not south west, and there are neither
hills nor caves. There is, however, a lesser known Cadnam. Now
known as Cadnam Ha, it is in the area of the Mendip Hills a few
miles from Chippenham. The entire area is riddled with caves, the
most famous one being Cheddar Gorge, which began as an enclosed
cave system but later collapsed. The earliest record of Cadnam is
1286, when it was spelt Cadenham, but of course it could be much
older.*)

HH   How do you get your food?

Morag The hounds hunt it.

HH   Are they your hounds?

Morag Yes, they are in my power.

HH   Have you some special power?

Morag I cure things.

HH   Are you some kind of a witch – a good witch?

Morag A wise woman.

HH   And you make people better? ... Do they come to your
         cave?

Morag They come to me from the settlement.

(*It is at fifty years old that I discover by chance through a routine
question that she had met Alfred.*)

HH   Do you know the year, or the name of the ruler of the
         land?

Morag Alfred was here ... they call him the Great.

(*I take her onward beyond her death at sixty-four but get no
response, so we turn back a little to the latter part of her life.*)

Morag The travellers have come back.

HH   And have they taken you with them?

Morag Yes ... travelling east (*a little time later*) ... We are
         hurrying to get to the walls ... London's walls ... We
         are going as fast as we can.

(*London is known to have been walled at this time.*)

         ... The Vikings are coming ... They are raiding the

country ... From the sea ... They come from Anglia.
*(Vikings raids were frequent in the south east around this time, and
they had already occupied Anglia.)*

Morag   ... They want to conquer the country. They are going
       to sack and burn it ... I don't think we shall make it ...
       They do not take prisoners ... setting fire to the wagon
       ... it is burned.

HH   Are you on foot?

Morag   Yes ... down in the grass ... lying still.

HH   Are you still alive?

Morag   I have got a knife in my back ... before I ran into the
       grass.

In the second interview, conducted about six weeks later, I
decided to concentrate on her royal patient, with further
investigation into the lifestyle the wise woman touched on the first
time around. So I took her immediately to the point where she
first meets Alfred's father, then King Ethelwulf and his sons. Her
age at this time is fifty.

Morag   Many visitors are coming today ... King Ethelwulf
       and his sons ... princes ... Ethelwulf ... He is the
       King of Wessex.

*(Ethelwulf ruled the land of Wessex from the year 839 until 856,
when he was demoted to ruler of the under kingdom of Kent
following his controversial second marriage. We will hear more of
that marriage later.)*

HH   What are his sons called?

Morag   Edward the Elder, Ethelbald, Ethelred and Alfred.

*(Edward the Elder was in fact a grandson of Ethelwulf, but the other
three are correct. Ethelwulf had another son, Ethelbert, and just a
few minutes later in the interview, as you will see, she manages to get
all four right. She does not mention a fifth son, Ethelstan, but
historians believe he died rather early on.)*

HH   Do you know the year?

Morag   I think it is 867.

(Sadly, she thinks wrong. Ethelwulf died in 858.)

Morag   I shall meet the King ... He has heard of me ... I
       sometimes cure people ... herbs and potions.

HH   Now, when you reach the settlement, I want you to tell
        me what it looks like. Will you do that?
Morag   Yes. The houses are made of wood and mud, a sort of
        clay hardened.
HH   What sort of wood, tree trunks?
Morag   Mostly oak ... logs and some planks.
HH   What shape are the houses, are they round or square
        or oblong?
Morag   They are mainly square and oblong ... Some are two-
        storeyed.
HH   And what shape is the roof, is it flat?
Morag   No, not quite flat. No ... it slopes to one side.
HH   And how many of these houses are there in the settle-
        ment?
Morag   About thirty or forty ... There is one large one in the
        middle ... It is a sort of meeting house ... A lot of the
        animals are kept in the houses with the people ... They
        have pigs and goats.
HH   Have you ever been inside one of the houses?
Morag   Not right inside.
HH   Do they have windows?
Morag   Yes ... They are just spaces in the walls. They have
        shutters that can be put up to them.
HH   And if you look through them, what is the floor made
        of?
Morag   A sort of hardened earth ... and there is a fire in the
        centre ... There are tables and stools ... wood.
HH   Do they have beds?
Morag   Yes ... sort of raised up from the ground slightly. They
        have a sort of mattress which goes on them – sort of
        reeds and rush matting.

*(The whole description seems very accurate. I thought she would be
wrong when she said some houses were two storeyed, but this is in
fact correct.)*

HH   And how do they get light at night?
Morag   They have reeds which burn.

*(This sounds like a description of the candles known to have been
used at this time. They were simply reeds dipped repeatedly in tallow
or even rendered animal fat. History books, however, seem to think*

oil lamps and some kind of torch were more common.)

HH   Is anyone in charge of the settlement?

Morag Yes.

HH   What is his rank?

Morag He is not called by rank; he is just called by name, but everyone obeys him.

HH   Now tell me what is happening at the settlement.

Morag There is quite a lot of excitement because of the visitors coming ... They are coming because there has been some trouble with the King's youngest son ... Alfred ... He is often ill.

HH   And are they bringing him to see you?

Morag Yes.

HH   Who told you?

Morag Athin when he came to the cave ... He is the head of the settlement.

HH   Does this settlement have a wall around it?

Morag It has a strong wooden fence ... to keep people out. They opened up the gates to let the visitors in.

HH   What does Ethelwulf look like? What colour is his hair?

Morag He is quite old ... dark.

(Ethelwulf is known to have lived to a relatively old age but because of Morag's inaccuracy of date we have no idea what stage in his life is being described now.)

Morag Ethelbald has fair hair ... He is about thirty or so.

HH   What are the names of his other sons?

Morag Ethelbert ... I should think about twenty-seven ... Ethelred, he has got red hair.

(Although she seems to claim none of the sons has been enthroned at this point, she gives them in exact order of their accessions. Therefore, as accession was, as nowadays, based on seniority, she has listed them in the correct order of their ages.)

HH   How old is Alfred?

Morag He is about twenty, I think.

(At the date she gives of around 867, Alfred would have been eighteen. However, she repeats her earlier inaccuracy about dates here. As I said, Ethelwulf had been dead some years in 867, and Alfred's three brothers would all have been King. Records show that

Ethelred had reigned for two years by this time.)
    HH   What colour is his hair?
    Morag He is not blond. It is not red, it is what you would call golden, I think.
    HH   What is the trouble with his health?
    Morag He suffers from constant pain ... stomach pains.
(Records tell that Alfred was in poor health. None of them actually say what was wrong with him, but modern researchers believe he may have been epileptic.)
    HH   And you can give him some medicine for that?
    Morag Yes.
    HH   Can you tell me the names of the herbs you would give him?
    Morag I cannot say. I cannot tell anyone what I use; it is not allowed. I make it into a liquid.
    HH   And it makes his stomach better?
    Morag Yes, but it won't cure it ... It can only be relieved; it cannot be cured. No one has put a name to it ... I feel I cannot cure it ... It needs some treatment I am not capable of giving ... He cannot sleep. It troubles him night and day and it is a great worry to Ethelwulf ... I will go back to the cave and prepare the medicine ... I was asked if I could cure Alfred of his affliction. But I have explained that he cannot be cured, but I can supply medicine as often as they need it.
    HH   What did Alfred say?
    Morag He said he would be glad to try anything to relieve it.
    HH   So what is happening to you now, Morag?
    Morag There is news of battles.
(The Saxons were at constant war with the Danes around this time.)
    HH   Did you take the medicine for Alfred?
    Morag Assa came for it.
(Again she is correct except for the dates – although records of dates in this period must not be taken to be absolutely accurate – in that Assa was a personal friend and tutor of Alfred. But there is no record of this relationship until 884, and as she is about to give her age as fifty-three, we assume it is now somewhere around 870.)
    Morag I have been supplying it for some time now ... He sends someone to fetch it.

(I assume by this that she slipped forwards some years when I asked her 'what is happening now?'.)

HH   How old are you now?

Morag Fifty-three.

HH   Anything exciting happening now?

Morag Mostly news of battles.

HH   What battles are these? Where is the fighting?

Morag It is quite a long way from here. Our news is that it is in Ashdowne.

(Here she is right in everything, including the date. The battle of Ashdowne was fought in 871.)

HH   Who is fighting in the battle?

Morag Ethelred and Alfred.

(They were indeed the only surviving sons of Ethelwulf at this time.)

HH   Who are they fighting?

Morag The Danes... They are always invading... They come across East Anglia.

HH   Are the Saxons beating the Danes in this battle, do you know?

Morag They win some of them; they lose some battles. At Ashdowne they are winning.

(Right again. The Danes, or Vikings, came out badly at Ashdowne.)

HH   Ethelwulf is still King?

Morag No ... Ethelred is King.

(871 was in fact the very end of Ethelred's reign over Wessex: Alfred was crowned some time in the same year.)

HH   Is Assa a man or woman?

Morag A man. He is Alfred's tutor ... Assa comes from Wales ... He was Bishop of St David's, but now he spends most of his time with Alfred.

(Assa Menevensis was from St David's on the western coast of Wales. He was a monk and later a bishop until he came to the court of Alfred. Apparently his terms of employment with Alfred included permission to return home at regular intervals.)

Morag He teaches Alfred Latin.

(This was Assa's main task in Alfred's court.)

Morag ends this fascinating interview by saying at the age of fifty-seven that Alfred is now King. Reckoning from her earlier references, the year must then be around 874, in which case Alfred has been on the throne about three years. Eight years later she says she is leaving her cave to be in London because Alfred is there.

In referring to the settlement in this interview, she called it not Cadnam but Catnium. There was a settlement of Roman origin on the Kent coast called Catnium, but it seems to me that this can be discounted in favour of a simple mispronunciation of Cadnam.

The third and final interview with Morag took place some thirteen months after the second. But despite this gap and my deliberate quick-fired questioning (in relative terms), she shows a startling consistency with our previous conversations, and gives a whole new set of facts about Alfred's family. This, needless to say, shows the clinical accuracy we have come to expect from Morag. Sadly, she also shows her confusion over dates right at the start, when I direct her back to the time of Ethelwulf's first visit. In this third interview, I asked her questions given to me by my researchers, based on their historical findings. The questions, to which the researchers already knew the correct answers, were given to me in a sealed envelope which I did not open until the interview had begun. This time she says she is aged 'forty something' rather than fifty as before. She says this time that Alfred is seventeen or eighteen. If we assume for a moment that the year is 867, as she said in interview number two, then her estimate of his age is right this time.

I thought at first I would test her medical knowledge. I knew one archaic term for an illness – ficus. Referring to haemorrhoids, it has not been used, to my knowledge, for centuries. But when I tried it on Morag, she gave, in what to us is quite an amusing way, a description of one of the side effects of haemorrhoids. She also told me that ficus was not Alfred's problem.

HH   How does it affect people?
Morag   They have to retire to the bushes ... because they are
        not well.
HH   Do they have to vomit? Or do they have looseness of
        the bowel?
Morag   They have looseness of the bowel.
HH   And does Alfred suffer from this?
Morag   I don't call it that.

HH   What do they call Alfred's illness? Do they have a
        name for it?
Morag   I don't know. I have never heard anybody call it.
HH   Do you know the name of Alfred's mother?
Morag   Osburgh.

*(Correct. Osburgh was Ethelwulf's first wife. He remarried very
late in life to a young girl named Judith, but there is no mention of
this from Morag at all. However, when I asked Sheila about this,
outside hypnosis, she said she had a recollection of Judith, but had a
feeling that the girl was never officially married to Ethelwulf. She
could remember being told at the time that she was simply the old
King's mistress.)*

HH   Did Alfred ever get married?
Morag   Yes ... Alswith.

*(Spellings vary from one record to another, but Alfred married
Elswitha in 868. From this and other answers, I assume she is
drifting in time, rather than anchoring on the point where I began the
interview.)*

HH   Did they have any children?
Morag   I think one that I know of ... Edward.

*(Alfred's son was Edward the Elder. This is the one Morag
accidentally got mixed up with Alfred's brothers in interview one.)*

HH   Did Alfred ever come to the cave to collect the
        medicine for himself?
Morag   No ... Someone else came ... Sometimes it was taken
        a long way across country ... Sometimes it was
        someone called Baldar. But once or twice it was Assa.
HH   What tongue does he speak?
Morag   I think he can speak many languages. I think he speaks
        Welsh, sometimes he speaks Latin, I think.
HH   How old was Alfred when he became King?
Morag   I think I heard it said he was twenty-two.

(Alfred was crowned at the age of twenty-one in the year 871.)

HH   And how old were you?
Morag   Maybe sixty something. I am not sure of my age ... No
        one told me my real age.

*(From the information she has already given, Morag was born
around 817. Thus she would be about sixty-four in the year of his
coronation.)*

HH   Assa collected the medicine for Alfred the first time?
Morag   Once or twice Assa came ... mostly somebody else ...
        I really only knew Balden ... I think he was a servant.
(*The nearest name I could find that was in use at the time was
Baldor, meaning bold. I found nothing to connect a man of that name
with any member of Alfred's court. Of course, it is not likely that one
would, as he was only a servant. At this point I ask her again the
order in which the family were crowned, and again she gets the
names and order correct. But then she adds something.*)
     Morag   There was a sister ... Ethelwith.
(*Alfred had a sister whom the history books call Ethelswitha.*)
     Morag   Ethelwith married the King of Mercia ... Burhed.
(*And she did indeed. Burhed was King of Mercia and he married
Alfred's sister in the year 853.*)
     HH   Burhed was King of Mercia?
     Morag   Yes.
     HH   What was Alfred king of?
     Morag   Wessex.
(*Correct, of course.*)
     HH   Did you actually see Alfred crowned King?
     Morag   No, he was crowned at Winchester.
(*Apparently, Winchester was the capital of Wessex. London was in
those days relatively insignificant.*)
     HH   Anything else to tell me that is unusual about Alfred
             and his father?
     Morag   They were fair skinned. Not like some of the Mercians
             that I met: they seemed to be darkish skinned.
(*This is a fairly widely known fact about the ethnic differences
between the predominantly Saxon people of Wessex and the more
Celtic Mercians.*)
     Morag   Ethelred had reddish hair, but Alfred was blond.
     HH   That's fine, Morag, now just relax.

There is one other fact about Alfred and his family which
Morag gave us, but which I have tried in vain to validate. And it is
most unfortunate, because it is the one fact she gave which is least
likely to be common knowledge in modern times. Sadly, that
same obscurity has confounded any attempt to trace it. For even if
we are to assume that it is true, it would have been so lacking in

consequence that no one would have bothered to record it. Even Assa himself, whose biographical works on his master are available to us has left a shroud of mystery over the little gem Morag left us. She says in the final interview that the whole family had a very distinctive cough. It was a sharp cough, she said, which seemed to afflict them most when they were eating. But she herself gives the reason why it was so insignificant: there was no illness at all, just this odd congenital quirk.

Nevertheless, Morag gave us more, both in quantity and accuracy, than we would ever have dared to hope for. Even allowing for the amazing powers of retention of the unconscious mind, I find it hard to accept that someone with Sheila's standard of historical education had ever heard so much detail on this one very limited subject. I am certain that, for anyone searching for the root cause of past life regression from my project, Morag is their guiding light. And to anyone with the pre-formed opinion that we are dealing simply with unconscious recall, our wise woman from the past may not be a cast iron case against their theories – but she certainly gives them a good run for their money.

But as well as the many facts Morag gives, let's think for a moment about one fact she does not. Think back to your own mental pictures of Alfred and the stories you have heard about him – or more precisely just the one story we all hear first. Nowhere in her entire recollection of the great man does she mention the anecdote about burning the cakes. And why should she? This is one of those silly stories that infants' school history lessons thrive on, but if we are really hearing the words of a contemporary of Alfred, what importance would such a person put on an incident of this kind? The barbarous Danes and the struggle for life were a daily reality to them. Who, in those circumstances, would want to be concerned with some spoiled cakes?

9
Separate Identities

By now, you will probably have decided for yourself which of the theoretical explanations of past life regression you find most acceptable. You do not have enough evidence to point a positive finger in any one direction, and what evidence I have given you may have been used emotively in order to reach your preferred conclusion. Yet you may be completely unshakeable in your belief. I envy you. The feeling that a mystery defies every form of explanation is a disquieting one, and the temptation is strong to seek not The Answer but any answer.

The reason for my envy is that I am still stuck with that restless discomfort of inconclusiveness. I have studied my evidence, and the evidence of the others before me, and all logical roads lead to a dark, shapeless vacuum with a question mark after it. It is as though someone had emptied the pieces of four jigsaw puzzles into a barrel, then shared out the well shaken result back into the four boxes. I see before me a portion of unquestionable evidence pointing towards one conclusion – but then there is another, equally beyond doubt, pointing the opposite way.

Before tackling the project, I had heard all the theories and explanations, and was prepared to give each one equal opportunity to prove itself. With the exception of the immediate dismissal of one theory (which I will deal with in the concluding chapter), I found little in the interview transcripts which could safely be said to bring out any particular one as favourite. But it was another source which, to me, pushed one of those possibilities very slightly to the fore. I am still far from certain, and the difference is only a marginal one. But if I were forced on threat of death to plump for just one, then the casting vote would go to reincarnation. Naturally, for anyone under threat of death this is a very comforting belief to hold, but the real reason would lie in what I have seen in the analysis of that part of the research which is the hardest for any subject, even unconsciously, to fake – the personality.

For every one of us, every move we make is dictated by a seemingly infinite permutation of character traits. These traits are as individual as fingerprints, yet many thousands of times more complex. Each one of us may think we have absolute freedom of choice, but how many of our everyday decisions are pre-determined by not what we want, but what we are. Many of our outward actions are universally known and used by us all in the assessment of the people around us. How we dress, walk, talk; what company we choose or shun; how we react in a crisis; all these are obvious clues to what we really are – clues that almost anyone can read. And anything so easily read can be faked with equal ease. But many clues can be found on a lower stratum where only the trained eye is privy to their meaning. And it is because these signals are so less widely known that they are more reliable. The subject under observation cannot either consciously or unconsciously alter what he is unaware of, and so these signals provide a more accurate means of analysis.

I had wondered for a long time, as I watched each regression subject slip back through the years, how much of the real self survived each apparent brush with the grave. After all, if at each turn of the wheel we are seeing a wholly new person, might we not also see a completely different personality? If there is no conscious memory of these lives prior to regression, then is it possible that the conscious characteristics of earlier lives can survive? The only answer I could get from studying past works was that this is perhaps the biggest of all the unexplored areas of the whole subject of past life regression.

Basically, each subject was given a test – a number of questions and tasks designed not only to analyse their personality profile, but also to quantify it in numerical terms which could be compared instantly with others.

The results showed one point instantly – that wherever each past life may come from or whatever its cause may be, it really is a totally different person we are talking to. Sadie Jewkes is not just Tina wearing a long dress. She is Sadie Jewkes. She is a woman in her own right, with her own thoughts and opinions, hopes and fears. Even if it could be proved after many more years of research that Sadie never existed in the nineteenth century, I have seen proof that she lives now.

But first, the experiment itself. For any personality profile analysis to be carried out partly within hypnosis, the first thing which must be done is to produce a compact format. Full analysis by conventional means would require some 600 questions to be posed to each subject. This is not practicable where hypnosis is involved, especially at the depths required for regression. Such an interrogation would prove far too tiring and very quickly make the subject restless. But for my purpose, the standard list could easily be distilled to about fifty with no sacrifice of accuracy or consistency. This figure, which includes such factual details as name, age and so on, was divided into two categories. The first measured the introversion/extroversion factor; the second dealt with the emotions, hopes and fears of the subjects in terms of their reactions to the things around them. Among the verbal questions in the first category, I put the request to draw a person of the subject's own sex, then one of the opposite. Not a very revealing exercise, you may think, but in the simple pencil drawings can be found a host of unconscious giveaways. To a trained observer, the stature of each figure and the relative stature of the two sexes, the clothes – if any – on the figures, even things like the size of the head and hands and the number of fingers, are all positive indicators of the many segments that go to make up a personality.

Each subject underwent the whole test twice – first in normal consciousness, then in regression under hypnosis. For the latter, I took each one back to the most recent life where they survived to their present chronological age. Thus the two 'people' could be made as similar as possible. They firstly had the same years of experience of life and, by picking the most recent, they lived in as similar worlds as possible. The nineteenth and early twentieth centuries in which the bulk of the most recent lives occurred were, although different in the more superficial ways, similar enough to the present day for the questions to have a common significance.

The answers and pictures were finally taken for analysis by two independent psychologists familiar with the format of the questionnaire. When I first saw their results, I realised that we had found something of extreme significance, but it was not until they were interpreted by more complex statistical means that I realised the extent of their revelation.

The initial result told me that every past character showed only twenty to twenty-five per cent similarity to the 'host' mind of the volunteer, with an overall average of twenty-three per cent. The figures not only showed a startling consistency from one subject to another, but also demonstrated beyond question that three-quarters of every character summoned by regression was totally unlike the living person who experienced it. Such an ample fraction as three quarters was more than I had dared hope for, but the findings of the next stage were more staggering by far. I began to wonder what result would be given if two completely separate living people were compared in the same way. Surely, by the laws of average and coincidence, any two people were bound to give some similar answers. It would be almost as unlikely for two people to give absolutely different answers in every case as it would for all their answers to be the same. This, I thought was bound to explain some of the remaining twenty to twenty-five per cent. So I asked the psychologists who had analysed the answers what this statistic would be. Given the questions I had used, two different people chosen at random – if socially and professionally similar – would show an overlap of twenty to twenty-five. This would suggest that the personalities of the present subjects and those they had in their past lives were not only different, but also had roughly the right amount of similarities to put those differences on a par with two living beings.

The fact that past lives seem totally independent in character from the minds they occupy can only strengthen the case of anyone believing they were once completely autonomous.

The existence of other completely separate personalities within each one of us – or certainly a vast proportion of us – as a permanent fixture, sets us a teasing philosophical question. Can these other minds be said to be 'alive' in the present? Any entity capable of sensory interpretation, emotion, opinion and memory can surely not be awarded any other status.

With regard to autonomy it has always been impossible to prove that a past life is autonomous without redress to a belief in certain of the theories. I believe that now that proof is much easier to find using only the objective evidence I have discovered, and although that proof may not be absolute, it is certainly an enormous step forward.

The first question which perhaps springs to mind on seeing the personality differences is, 'what about Karma?' Now that we know there is a significant shift in character from one life to the next, can we show that there is a process of purification or refinement along the way? The question is an obvious and logical one, but I feel the answer cannot come from the mortal mind. In order to include such a question in a scientific analysis, it would first be essential to quantify every known moral standard and assess even the tiniest human reaction not only into the language of fact but even into numerical form. When two people in the same branch of the same denomination of the same faith cannot reach agreement on what is right and wrong, what hope has a mere scientist? There is a point, even in the most advanced of scientific studies, where one must step down, without fear of being thought cowardly, and say, 'That is not a question for man'.

10
Conclusion

Somewhere along the line between eternity and daydream lies the seed of an answer. It is the answer to the vexing puzzle that asks: why does every head seem to carry more than one mind, every soul more than one name? That line is the one which links all of the theories ever put forward in the bid to explain the past life regression phenomenon. Some observers may look to the eternity end of the line. They will say we are witnessing the process of a spiritual continuum as a soul repeatedly cloaks itself in earthbound form.

Others, favouring the other end of the line, will tell you the unconscious mind appears to have taken up a hobby. It has turned its idle moments to amateur scriptwriting, with a leaning towards historical fiction. They might explain that the internal flair for the unreal serves a very real function – to help the conscious mind to come to terms with reality. They see the role of the apparent past lives – whether they are ever relived by the conscious or not – as something similar to that of an ordinary dream.

Each one of those theories was examined at the beginning of the project on the basis of existing evidence, and can be now viewed again in the very different light of the new findings.

Everyone on earth, with the possible exception of children, who are too young to comprehend the instruction, and the certified insane, who have lost their grasp of reality, can be hypnotised to some degree. The many who at first are only capable of undergoing light hypnosis can be taken far deeper with patience and careful conditioning. The same applies at the next level, where some are immediately receptive to the deep trance state, whilst others need more time and effort. This is the state necessary for anyone who is to experience past life regression, but again it is not immediately available to everyone. Taking any random group as I did, there appears to be a ten per cent chance that an individual can reach the desired stage without delay. But this figure is considerably higher – indeed far nearer to one hundred per cent – in circumstances where time available and effort to be expanded are unlimited.

So it is important to realise before we examine our findings more closely that we are talking about a phenomenon which touches almost everyone on earth. The science fiction writer Arthur C. Clarke says in the introduction to his book *2001 A Space Odyssey* that behind every man and woman on earth stand twenty-eight ghosts, for that is the proportion of those living now to those who have ever lived. Perhaps we should now qualify the author's claim by adding that at least some of those ghosts are not behind; they are within. It is sad to think that, with a total world population of well over three billion, there may well be fifteen or even twenty billion past life experiences which will never be tapped by hypnosis. This does not mean, of course, that they will never be revealed in any other way. The members of the world's large Buddhist population seem not only to have spontaneous recall of their past lives but are also quite convinced that they are just that – past lives every bit as real as the present ones.

But, to return to those who can be regressed easily, there was one more factor I found which governed the final selection of the top subjects. The fact that regression can be achieved without much difficulty in a particular volunteer is by no means the end of the search. Beyond that, I found two completely different types of regression, different both in nature and in the validity of the results. What you have read of the fascinating lives of five women has surfaced in their minds along with tears of sadness and joy, groans of agony, and light-hearted laughter. But there have been other cases where all the potentially exciting revelations were recounted with no more emotional involvement than one would expect from reading a drab and badly written novel. The difference between these two types of regression, however, goes far beyond their apparent audience-value, for the emotional involvement seems to carry with it a much broader band of validity. Where I have seen the tears and heard the laughter, I have known what would lie in the replies from the various archives where validation was sought. These and these alone are the regressions which convince one that we are dealing not with mere fantasy but that we have found the route to something else. This is not to say that the non-emotive variety are composed entirely of fantasy, simply that the degree of reality is well below the threshold where the evidence is adequate to show any real proof of credibility. This is possibly related to the depth of hypnosis achieved by the subject on the occasion.

It is interesting to note that during the screening process which led to the selection of the best volunteers, a number of seemingly less likely signs also showed themselves as indicating which were likely to be the most fruitful. Why, for example, should people with blue eyes seem more adept at looking into the past? Or why should the right-handed have a better grasp of their earlier lives? Such links between the individual's physical attributes and ease of entering hypnosis are not known in the world of conventional hypnotherapy, these traits appeared to be relevant in the case of my regressions. The best subjects for regression, it now seems, are female, aged thirty-five to forty-five, have blue eyes and are right-hand dominant. Even more oddly, they avert their eyes to the left rather than the right when asked an embarrassing or intimate question.

These factors may seem on the whole too superficial to be the basis for any real practical purpose, but in any future selections I make I will certainly take them all into consideration.

But these matters, for all their value, are only means to an end. They simply helped to streamline an investigation of such wide range without cutting any corners, while keeping the overall time spent within practical limits. What then of the actual findings they helped to produce? Let us first examine each theory as I saw it at the beginning of the research, and the factors which lend credibility to each in the eyes of its supporters. Of the six main contenders, three can be placed in the category of conventional science, i.e. they are based entirely on accepted scientific fact; the fourth is scientific speculation; and the remaining two are in the realms of theology and the occult. Though the more conservative usually settle on one of the first three, the first one is the favourite of the out-and-out sceptic, as it requires no theorising at all.

Purposeless fantasy. A need of the unconscious mind to tell

stories to itself. Devotees of this theory say there is no reason or logic: it simply happens.

Therapeutic fantasy. In the same way that our every day emotions of hope and fear are fed back to us in symbolic form as we dream, a similar role is attributed to these apparent past lives. The idea is that, as in dreams, we can project our fantasies and fears into a fictitious scenario where they can do no harm to the real world.

Cryptamnesia. As one might guess by its 'jargonese' title, this one is the favourite in the world of conventional psychology. In this case, the fantasy is unearthed as if it were buried treasure, deposited many years before by the mind of a child facing the need to grow up into reality, yet unwilling to part completely with its childlike daydreams. The existence of cryptamnesia in the conventional form is now widely accepted, but it is only relatively recently that it has been put forward as an explanation of past life regression. Psychologists believe a child's fascination with the past becomes interwoven with fantasy, but as the child approaches adulthood these fantasies become buried in the unconscious, rather than being abandoned altogether.

Genetic Memory and Ancestral Recall are two terms describing what is effectively the same phenomenon. We can all see the physical equivalent of this around us and even in ourselves every day. We may have our mother's brown eyes or grandfather's distinctive nose; may we not inherit also a small slice of their memory? And, as the physical characteristics originate from countless generations back, could not this family share-out of the mental filing cabinet have an equally long reach through time? Evidence of genetic memory is still sparse in orthodox research and far from conclusive. It is, however, a subject which more and more people are beginning to take seriously, and one which justifies a great deal of research in its own right. Before you begin to fall too strongly for genetic memory as a possible explanation of past life regression, I should point out that this is the one theory which can be disproved absolutely for reasons which I shall come to very soon.

Spirit possession or mediumship are two separate explanations which are close enough in content to be considered as one. In the same way as a spiritualist medium appears to fall into a spontaneous state of trance while summoning what are claimed to be spirits of the dead, it could be said that the deep hypnotic trance needed for regression could produce the same ability to bridge the void. A similar theory suggests that the mind of a living person may attract a number of spirits which take up permanent residence in or around the head. Through their connection with the living person, it is suggested, they could then use the trance state, as in the mediumship theory, to take temporary possession of those parts of the mind which reach the outside world.

Reincarnation. It is odd that I have had to avoid that word when seeking validation evidence from clerical sources, for it is only quite recently that ecclesiastical doctrine has taken a stand against reincarnation. The history of the faith in Britain, and indeed the whole world, shows quite clearly that the church in the past considered it as a valid and respectable possibility. Up to very few centuries ago it was quite acceptable and proper to see reincarnation not as an alternative to the Kingdom of Heaven but rather as a detour on the way. After all, those religions which accept reincarnation as an integral doctrine, do nonetheless see heaven as the finishing point. Though we may come back into tangible earthly form a number of times – not always as human beings, many believe – these visits are seen as merely brief stops in preparation for a later eternity. The whole world is seen in this theory as a huge classroom, where the lesson is perfection, and each life's experiences take one a step nearer, just as in the annual moving up by one form at school.

If what we are seeing is reincarnation, then we are speaking directly with the souls of many past lives, each one as real as the present, and each with its own individuality and environment, its own feelings, its own reason for being.

It is almost possible to predict from the character of an observer which of these theories he or she is likely to favour. It is not only psychologists who tend to cling to a predetermined belief. Sceptical or credulous, open-minded or dismissive, theologist or humanist, there is a theory somewhere there which is tailor-made just for you. I wonder how many people have reached a conclusion on first hearing of past life regression and then actually changed their mind after learning more of the facts. It is my guess that the group is a small and very exclusive one. If you do not belong to that group, then I beg of you to open your mind before reading on. I am in no doubt that the findings of the last three years have a very real bearing on every one of the theories, and that is a view shared by every member of the research team who has inspected the results along with me.

We have seen over and over again how the regressed mind dwells often on the irrelevent trivia which on the one hand are left virgin by the history books but, conversely, are impossible to disprove. From the speckled history of Mary Morrison's employment record to Andromache's attempts as a tour guide, each revelation and the analysis of the reasons behind it may throw a slightly different light on one's feelings about the phenomenon without producing a concrete conclusion. But from a close examination of the interviews and validations as a whole, it is possible to establish certain hard factual conclusions in many areas formerly supported only by tentative belief. Here now are some of those findings (readers may be able to deduce others) and their sources in the transcripts of the interview:

1) At least three of the five subjects had at least one life in which they died without issue. I do not propose in this list to relate these findings to the later conclusions, but the answer which these terminated blood-lines give to the theory of genetic memory is, to my mind, both overwhelming and final. The most obvious one here is Irene, whose most recent life ended at the age of six. Tina's Mary Kaye/Morrison lost her first child and was left sterile by the birth complications. Sheila's Jeanette Cartier was drowned in her teens while still single, living with her family and making no mention of what in those times would be a scandal. Many others make no reference to children but describe circumstances where they might exist, so absolute proof could not be claimed.

2) No two lives overlap. In every single case from my own files, all the lives of each subject occupy different periods of time. In some cases the gap between may become very short – as short as two years in the project – but no one has managed two simultaneous lives.

3) No connection can be found between the periods of history occupied by a subject's lives and any historical interest the subject may have had. Where, for example, Sheila had learnt some Tudor history at school, her four lives occur at apparently random

periods. Her second life, as Elizabeth De Bois, does spill slightly into the beginning of the House of Tudor, but the overlap is minimal and such an early part of a royal house would show little of the characteristics by which we would know it.

4) The same applies to any possibility of geographical connections. In fact, a correlation of all the areas in which the past lives were based shows quite the opposite. With the exception of Sheila, who lived in Portsmouth until she was seventeen, all the principal subjects have been brought up exclusively in the north and north east of England. Yet, for some totally inexplicable reason, the bulk of their lives originate in the south and south west. To take the point a little further, none of the five has any other connections, such as relatives, with any of the specific areas of their respective past lives.

I should perhaps mention a small matter here which relates to another theoretical explanation of past life regression once held by some, but now almost entirely discarded. It was felt at one time, when subjects in regression produced facts they did not consciously know, that there could be some kind of telepathic link with the hypnotist. I have personally never given this theory much credibility, but for those who may see it as a viable alternative I have made one further brief check. Any form of elimination based on the subjects, e.g. lack of geographical connections, may now be read as applying to me also.

5) Whatever theory we may attribute to the phenomenon, the unconscious mind seems to be in little doubt about the answer. In conversations with the subject's unconscious, I have found each one very aware of a continuity of time which appears to connect their lives. In cases where patients under therapy have regressed spontaneously, that regression has come out of a very definite backwards movement. During the normal scan of the present life, they will float gently backwards towards birth, then after a pause seem to find their other selves waiting at an earlier point in time. Also consider the answers of the virgin soul; she seemed to need no convincing about where her life was going and where it came from.

Of course, much of this could be explained by conscious intervention. Instead of believing the unconscious is privy to information from sources other than the outside world (some kind of instinct?) one could simply say it is feeding off the wishful thinking of the conscious mind. But this is parried by the mixed opinions of the volunteer group, who are far from believing solidly in reincarnation. I can add very little weight to this argument by quoting the very positive answers gained during the screening under hypnosis. Every subject, with the obvious exception of the virgin soul, gave an immediate 'yes' to the question, 'have you lived before?' but I freely concede the question is a leading one and, although very useful in cataloguing, cannot be used as any kind of proof.

6) Are the various life stories already complete in the subjects' heads before they are brought out by regression? My answer to this can only be yes. The speed with which every little detail is summoned, and the fact that it fits perfectly into the story around it, can lead to no other conclusion. Not even an accomplished fiction writer could instantly compose a story in which every cross-reference slots so neatly into the part of the plot where it belongs. Notice for example, where one life has undergone more than a single interview, how the fresh information in subsequent sessions interlocks perfectly with the first.

7) This relates closely to the next positive observation: that there is a staggering degree of consistency between two interviews, even when, as in many cases, well over a year elapsed between the two conversations. Over and over again, I deliberately covered the same ground in the second and third interviews with one past life, and over and over again came the same remarkably consistent answers. There were obvious exceptions, most of them concerning mistakes too blatant to camouflage, but these were very much the exception. These two observations, of consistency and the almost instant recital of fact, prove to me beyond doubt that hypnosis and the invitation to recall have no part whatsoever in the origin of these hidden autobiographies. Even though only a tiny fraction of them will ever be brought to light, I am sure that they are there now – in you, in me, in probably almost everyone. Within each of us, the book is already written; it is simply waiting to be opened and read.

It is both highly unethical and, one would assume, extremely difficult to put a very small child under hypnosis, but it seems clear from these findings that if anyone were to find a way of investigating these young minds they would find a full set of past life experiences every bit as clear as those we have seen.

Another point in favour of this conclusion is the stubbornness with which the subjects seem to hold on to their facts. Even in the face of persistent argument, their behaviour throughout is that of someone who knows a fact for certain and will defend its accuracy down to the last irrelevant detail. Remember how Hazel's Mary Gates almost put up a fight about the year of her birth? I insisted that if she were fifteen years old in 1810, then she would have been born in 1795. But '1796' was the stern, unshakeable answer, and Mary was having it no other way. Of course, if her birthday had not yet come that year, then she was right and I was wrong.

Surely, if these things we have heard were made up on the spot, or even made up at all, there would be no need for all this argument, particularly as in such a deep trance state such a disagreement would require a significant amount of effort. I know that this one factor in itself cannot be seen as conclusive, but I still cannot help but feel that a mere story teller would opt for the quiet life and simply agree.

8) Under regression to a certain age in a past life, the subjects show no knowledge whatsoever of the things they learned later in that life. This is particularly pronounced in the childhood stages. How many of the ten year olds in the interviews do not know their exact address, their father's Christian name or even the name of the monarch? Yet in almost every case, as I slide them forwards in years they can recall every one of these facts instantly.

9) The next observation seems at first to contradict the last. Although a second thought shows that it does not, it still leaves a teasing paradox. On a few occasions when the subjects have been returned to normal consciousness following a regression interview, they have made the same curious comment. They can recall being the person of their past life and remember that person's feelings. But they also say the person from the past was able to read some of their own present thoughts. They add that these twentieth century visions, superimposed on their very different world, would fill them at first with a confusion which took quite some getting used to, and made the forming of an answer at times difficult.

This was also the cause, you may recall, of Irene's reluctance to marry while she was Alison the Gipsy girl. Instead of thinking of her own bridegroom and the pleasure of married life in store, this poor girl was faced with a dilemma. She could not be unfaithful to a man who would not be born until many centuries hence. Little wonder the girl asked to be brought back, especially when one considers the Gipsy attitude towards adultery. Any trespass outside the bounds of marriage by a Gipsy woman of that time would have ended not in the courts but at the stake.

10) The memories of past lives appear to be present at various levels of consciousness. Though they cannot be brought out in full until a proper deep trance has been established, it would not be true to say that they exist at this level exclusively. In fact, my first meeting with all of the lives related here came while the volunteers were in very light hypnosis at the early stages, while I was preparing the catalogue of the lives I could later expect to examine in full.

What can it be that we are seeing? Normal twentieth century human beings remembering lives from further back than their minds might even conceive? A playful segment of the inner mind? Or a floating spirit seeking communication through a borrowed body?

Perhaps the best path to some hint of an answer lies not in what we can prove, for that is still comparatively very little, but by the elimination of that which fails to prove itself.

Could we expect for example that a gathering of spirits from the dead would have any reason to avoid overlapping themselves in one head? Why should the ghost of a short life associate itself with a ghost whose life followed closely, while the ghost of a long life did not?

What of fantasy? The amount of information needed in one mind to conjure up validated facts surrounding a life-that-never-was must be beyond calculation. The same applies to 'therapeutic fantasy', but in that theory lies a bigger question. With such a mixture of mostly humdrum existences, can anyone see any experience recounted in any one of the interviews which might hold some steadying or reassuring value to the present day subjects, as one would expect from any regression for therapeutic purposes? In fact, there was no apparent change in personality behaviour patterns by any of the subjects throughout the programme which might have been attributed to some therapeutic effect of the experimental regressions.

Can any believer in cryptamnesia as the cause attribute all the things we have seen to the mind of a child? The disgust of Elizabeth De Bois as a drunken suitor wants to take her outside; the sickening yet accurate description of death by smallpox; the need to escape poverty by marriage; these would all have had to come from daydreams of a child if we are to keep cryptamnesia in the race.

Are we then really seeing some surviving vestige of lives past, whether by rebirth or any other medium? This is the question which calls for the findings of the personality profile analysis. The possibility that we may be hearing words of someone who really lived, seems strongly suggested by the results. How else, you may ask, can one mind contain three or four or even five, completely separate personalities? One would think that if the 'lives' had been conceived within that mind they would show strong character traits giving clues to their origin. But no, the results show quite the opposite. Even to the extent of producing a credible random element, they tell us that the 'lives' and their host minds are no more likely to show similarities than are the minds of a landlady and her lodgers. Perhaps we could learn a great deal by taking the analogy a little further. The landlady's lodgers differ from her own family only in that they have not grown up with her. Their formative period may have happened many miles away, although they now live in the same house. This is the most powerful point made by the personality profiles. Are we dealing with a subject's 'own family' or 'lodgers'? If the profiles had proved to be 'family', then this would obviously favour those theories based on some form of made up life created within the head rather than entering the mind in a fully-formed condition. Similar personalities in the past and present lives would clearly show that, like a family, they had grown up with their host. But as the results show the exact opposite, they seem to indicate that they were already intact on entering the mind of the host. To my mind, the personality profile results are the most convincing scientific findings I have ever seen which offer proof that some part of all of us is eternal. This does not automatically mean that we have pinned down some tangible and absolute proof of reincarnation, but of all the factors pointing in every direction, it seems that rather more of them point that way than any other. However, there is still one large and seemingly insurmountable obstacle in the path of that belief. If this were simply reincarnation with nothing else added, then why does every regression researcher not have validation of every word, at least for the more recent lives? I have said many times that, whatever the principal source may be, there is unquestionably a sprinkling of fantasy thrown in apparent random around the traceable facts. I accept that this might throw a proportion of the validation searches off course, but surely it could not disprove the theory of former existence, in the light of the available evidence.

One of the fundamentals of the quest, as I have already explained, is not only to pinpoint a single explanation but also to seek a more positive conclusion to the question of whether what we are seeking has its cause outside the realms of known science. Since the beginning of my own programme, investigators of the subject in the U.S.A. have released startling new findings which close the lid on this question tighter than ever before.

For anyone favouring the more down to earth explanations of the regression phenomenon, perhaps the hardest thing to accept would be that a subject in a past life could be capable of greater or wider perception than in present life. We have seen from every researcher of the subject how strongly this line has been followed in terms of historical or geographical fact. This in itself is not entirely foolproof, and neither are simple tests of mental ability. For we know very well that the mind's potential, both in agility and in the recall of experience, is far greater at the unconscious level. Within those parts of the mind, one who has never visited a certain area may, it is argued, have a storehouse of informaton about it locked away. The non-mathematician may also possess untapped ability to calculate, the non-artist may well be hiding at the back of his mind a flair for artistic creativity. But do the blind know how to see?

At the level of existing knowledge about the mind, the answer must unequivocally be NO. Even with the unconscious mind unveiled by a deep state of hypnosis, the congenitally blind, i.e. those who have never seen – show absolutely no grasp of visual conception. Not even the mind's eye of imagination can, it seems, give a passable imitation of the reality of sight.

Yet to these American researchers it has been shown that such blind people have 'eyes' within them – far deeper within than the so-called mind's eye. According to their results, the interviews with past lives of the congenitally blind show every bit as much visual imagery as those of the normally sighted. Such exclusively 'sighted' experiences as a stain on wood, a ship on the horizon or a grubby garment appear as clear in their narratives as they would from anyone with the most perfect vision. For the first time in their life, they utter, completely without prompting, such phrases as 'I see' just as naturally as they have always described touch, smell, sound, or taste. Indeed, they show all the signs of a very deep involvement with these new found experiences of sight. 'He's got blotches on his skin,' 'She looked sloppy in a dirty blouse,' 'The whole thing (a wooden bedpost) appeared water-stained,' and even, 'Her eyes were brown, a particular shade of brown,' all flow quite naturally from the lips of those who have never, ever, seen. Notice that these are not only visual experiences but those from which no clues overlap via the other senses. A rough looking stone will also feel rough, a gravel path will give away its nature by the sound underfoot. But who can feel the colour of an eye?

The American researchers, having travelled roughly the same road as myself had, like me, arrived at the same conclusion – that the only theory which cannot be dispelled is that of reincarnation. One cannot disprove it, but can one prove it?

With courage, they took the congenitally blind, many of whom could not even distinguish light from shade, and regressed them into an earlier time where they were able to see a world they had never seen. Returned to the present, they were blind again.

Did those people really see while their minds were given flight? In absolute terms we may never know, but consider, before you reach your own conclusion, the side effect suffered by these subjects long after the experiments were finished. Many of them became depressed when thinking back to their time in regression. When asked why, they simply said that they had realised fully, and for the first time, exactly what it is they were born without. In other words, they now knew what they were missing. And they seemed to know it very well.

I hope I can say that I have helped to pave the way for future researches, including further sojourns of my own, but I would be wrong to claim I have found the answer of answers. A few ·certainties have been established but, by the same token, the process has illuminated a wealth of new question marks.

You can make a candle, then make fire to light it, then hold it up to shed light on the hidden writings in the dark corners. But then, as the light flickers on the words for the first time, you discover that they offer no answers – only more searching questions.